TELL 'EM I DIED GAME

GRAHAM SEAL

TELL 'EM I DIED GAME

THE LEGEND OF NED KELLY

HYLAND
HOUSE

ERRATUM

At the end of page 91, insert the following two lines:

eastern Victorian society. But it would need a 'colonial stratagem' to effect
the necessary changes.

This edition first published in 2002 by
Hyland House Publishing Pty Ltd
PO Box 122
Flemington, Victoria 3031

An earlier edition of this text was published by
Hyland House as *Ned Kelly in Popular Tradition* in 1980.

Cataloguing-in-Publication entry:

Seal, Graham, 1950- .
   Tell 'em I died game : the legend of Ned Kelly.

   Bibliography.
   Includes index.
   ISBN 1 86447 047 X.

   1. Kelly, Ned, 1855-1880 - Legends. 2. Bushrangers -
   Australia - Biography. I. Seal, Graham, 1950- Ned Kelly in
   popular tradition. II. Title.

364.155092

Edited by Bet Moore
Design and layout by Rob Cowpe Design
Printed by McPherson's Printing Group, Victoria, Australia

FOREWORD TO THE FIRST EDITION
(Ned Kelly in Popular Tradition)

The morning of the eleventh of November will always be a special time for Australians. They recall how on that day in 1975 the prostitution of the Commonwealth constitution was procured by politicians at the hands of a complaisant viceroy. They can never forget that on that day in 1918 there ended the vast slaughter, in which their volunteer soldiers suffered more grievously, relative to the number engaged, than the men of any other army: and they will always remember how at that time in 1880 Ned Kelly was hanged to become the first figure in the mythology of his countrymen.

The deification of Kelly began long before his execution. Songs, ballads and orally transmitted yarns were made about his exploits, real and imaginary, almost as soon as they took place. Contemporary newspaper stories often praised the Kellys—if only in a backhanded fashion, by contrasting their superb bushmanship with the flat-footed ineptitude of the colonial police forces. After Glenrowan Ned's magnificent performance in the final trial scene assured him of a good press. Who can ever forget the last solemn words of the presiding judge, Sir Redmond Barry: 'Edward Kelly, I hereby sentence you to death by hanging. May the Lord have mercy on your soul.' Or the outlaw's confident reply that he would meet his fellow Irishman in hell: 'Yes, I will meet you there!' Or the fact that Barry died unexpectedly twelve days later?

It is safe to say that every one of the hundred years since then has contributed something to the Kelly legend — a new song, story, play, poem, painting or folk-tale. Up till about the time of World War II most of the material belonged to folk or popular culture. It proliferated often in spite of the efforts of officials and school-teachers to suppress it, and it flourished in every state and in city and country areas alike.

There were dozens of cheap pamphlets, luridly bound and written, some of which never found their way into any bibliography — like 'true histories' of the Kelly gang written 'by Dan Kelly, supposedly shot at Glenrowan.' There was the first feature-film in the world's history, made in Australia of course and about what else than the life and death of Ned Kelly? And there were doggerel ballads, poetically contemptible but, none the less popular for that, like this evocation of Ned's image during the war with Japan.

Ned Kelly was a gentleman:
Many hardships did he endure.
He battled to deprive the rich,
Then gave it to the poor.
But his mode of distribution
Was not acceptable to all,
Though backed by certain gunmen
Known as Gilbert and Ben Hall.

I think it was a pity
They hanged him from a rope.
They made Australian history
But they shattered Kelly's hope.
If they'd sent him into Parliament
His prospects would be bright.
He'd function for the masses
If not for the elite.

And perhaps now in Australia
We'd have millions trained with him,
All laughing with a vengeance
At the little yellow men.
If Ned and such guerillas
Were with us here today
The Japs would not be prowling round
New Guinea and Milne Bay.

Since Ned went over the Border
There has been many a change.
Yet we may adopt his tactics
Around the Owen Stanley Range.
Poor Ned, he was a gentleman
But never understood.
We want men of such mettle now
To stem the yellow flood!

Since the war the Kellys have been more firmly enshrined than ever in popular culture, but they have become the leading symbols of Australian nationalism in 'high culture' also. The Kelly legend is the most important theme in the work of our greatest living painter, Sidney Nolan, and the subject of what is arguably our greatest drama, certainly our greatest verse-play, Douglas Stewart's *Ned Kelly*. It is surprising that Patrick White has not yet written on the subject.

The Kellys' pre-eminence in our mythology is signified most clearly, if also most dully, by their inclusion in the history books. Since E. G. Shann's *Economic History of Australia* (1930), no 'general' history of this country has been complete without some significant reference to bushranging and the Kelly gang, and in the last few years there have been a dozen or more 'serious' books devoted solely to the Kellys. Most of them, unfortunately, take themselves, in a certain sense, too seriously.

As historians their authors set out, above all, to establish 'the facts' and to disentangle the facts from the vast jungle of legend which surrounds them. This endeavour leads inevitably to barren and boring disputation about what 'the facts' were. Were Ned Kelly, Dan Kelly, Steve Hart and Joe Byrne cold-blooded murderers or chivalrous heroes, brutal thugs or the champions of the rural poor? It is a barren argument because it cannot be answered in 'either–or' terms and because the answer is not very important anyway.

Of course most bushrangers were brutal thugs, though they usually murdered only policemen and people despised even more deeply by most Australians last century—police informers. Of course too most of them took some trouble to pose as patriotic Australians and friends of the poor, because it paid them to do so. The career of those who did not was very short. Without the support of 'bush telegraphs', free selectors and other poor country-folk, they were usually caught and tried in days rather than months or years.

But the answer is unimportant because, in the matter of bushranging, it is not in the least 'the facts' but the mythology to which they gave rise which should interest the historian and all the rest of us. To know certainly whether the Kellys murdered the policemen Kennedy, Scanlon and Lonigan in cold blood, or shot them 'in fair fight', would teach us nothing significant about our history or ourselves; but to understand why our ancestors generally insisted on lionising bushrangers teaches us a great deal.

Professor J. D. Molony is currently writing, I am told, what I think will be a great book on the Kellys. It is said that this book will cast grave doubt on the authenticity of Ned Kelly's Jerilderie Letter, the stirring document said to have been given by Ned to a terrified bankclerk of that town. To my mind it matters no more whether Ned 'wrote' —or dictated—the letter, than it does whether Shakespeare, Bacon or a person unknown wrote the greatest plays in our language. In semiliterate but highly poetic words the Jerilderie Letter expresses perfectly what the Kellys and all bushrangers *were believed* to be fighting for. To understand how and why and when most Australians came to sympathise with the sentiments of the Jerilderie Letter is to understand a great deal of importance in our history. To know the extent to which Ned Kelly himself, or any other bushranger, 'really' believed in these sentiments is interesting, but not very important.

That is why I think Graham Seal's book the best yet published on the Kellys. Though a serious and scholarly work, it is written in a clear and lively style. Though concerned to establish the 'facts' of the Kelly story, it is not *too* concerned about them. It *is* concerned to trace and explain the growth of the Kelly legend and this is what matters most, or ought to matter most, to all of us.

Russel Ward
UNIVERSITY OF NEW ENGLAND
6 MARCH 1980

CONTENTS

LIST OF ILLUSTRATIONS

ACKNOWLEDGMENTS

In addition to those who assisted with the first edition of this book, I thank them again and add my gratitude to others for assistance with the second:

Phyl and Geri Lobl, Charles Pickett; Ivor Hemphrey; Geoffrey Kleem; Wendy Lowenstein; Russel Ward; John McQuilton; Patrick O'Farrell; the Archives Office of New South Wales; the Victorian State Library; the Australian National Library; the National Film Archives (now Screensound Australia); the Burke Museum, Beechworth; the British Library in London and Boston Spa; the Leeds City Library; the Vaughan Williams Memorial Library of the English Folk Dance and Song Society; the archives of the Institute of Dialect and Folk Life Studies at the University of Leeds; Stewart Sanderson; Tony Green; Anne Beggs-Sunter of the University of Ballarat; Bert and Gwenda Davey; Michael Schoo of Hyland House; Professor John Widowwson, National Centre for English Cultural Tradition, University of Sheffield; the various copyright holders who granted permission to reproduce their words or images; and, as always, my family.

I should like to thank the Sydney Bush Music Club for permission to use the tunes given in *Six Authentic Songs From The Kelly Country*, compiled by John Meredith in 1955, for 'The Bold Kelly Gang', 'Stringybark Creek' and 'Farewell to Greta'; Ure Smith and the authors for permission to use 'Bold Ben Hall', 'Farewell Dan and Edward Kelly', 'Kelly Was Their Captain', 'The Kelly Gang' and 'Ye Sons of Australia' from

Folksongs of Australia by John Meredith and Hugh Anderson; Angus and Robertson for permission to reprint 'We're The Jolliest Lot of Thieves' and 'Farewell to Greta' from *Old Bush Songs* by D. Stewart and N. Keesing as well as 'The Mystery Man' and 'The Death of Morgan' from *Australian Bush Ballads* by the same authors.

Thanks are also due to Dover Publications, USA for permission to quote from Professor F. J. Child's *The English and Scottish Popular Ballads*; Crown Publications, New York, for the use of 'Jesse James' from B. Botkin's *A Treasury of American Folklore*; Oxford University Press for the use of 'Brennan on the Moor' and 'Turpin Hero' from *Cecil Sharp's Collection of English Folksongs* edited by M. Karpeles; Rigby (Australia) for the use of 'Bold Jack Donahue' and 'Ned Kelly Was an Irishman' from Ron Edward's *Big Book of Australian Folksong, Stringybark & Greenhide* and Brad Tate for 'We Are Two Plucky Troopers' and Warren Fahey for permission to quote from *Joe Watson: Australian Traditional Folksinger*, to use 'My Name is Edward Kelly', and a verse of 'Farewell Dan and Edward Kelly'. The proprietors of the *Sydney Morning Herald* granted permission to reproduce any extract from their publication. Walter S. Heard kindly allowed reproduction of the still from the film *When The Kellys Were Out*, as did the proprietors of the Melbourne *Herald* for W. M. Hughes' article, 'A Bright Weekend in Jerilderie'. Penguin Books gave permission for the use of 'Ned Kelly Was A Gentleman' from the *Penguin Book of Australian Ballads,* edited by Russel Ward.

MAIN EVENTS 1854–81

November or December 1854 Ned Kelly born.

October 1869 Ned Kelly acquitted of assault and robbery charges.

May–June 1870 Charged with aiding bushranger Harry Power. Acquitted.

October 1870 Convicted of violent assault and of sending indecent letters to a female — six months' hard labour.

27 March 1871 Released from Beechworth Gaol — two months' remission for good behaviour.

May 1871 Convicted of receiving a stolen horse — three years' hard labour.

February 1874 Released from Pentridge.

September 1877 Fined for being drunk and disorderly and for resisting and assaulting the police in the execution of their duty.

15 April 1878 Fitzpatrick incident.

9 October 1878 Mrs Kelly sentenced to three years' hard labour.

26 October 1878   Stringybark Creek.

1 November 1878   Ned and Dan Kelly, Steve Hart, and Joe Byrne outlawed.

9–10 December 1878   Euroa raid (Cameron Letter).

2 January–22 April 1879   Sympathisers gaoled.

8–10 February 1879   Jerilderie raid (Jerilderie Letter).

26–28 June 1880   Glenrowan battle, Ned Kelly captured. Dan Kelly, Steve Hart, and Joe Byrne killed.

28–29 October 1880   Ned Kelly's trial.

11 November 1880   Ned Kelly's execution.

23 November 1880   Judge Redmond Barry died.

December 1880–April 1881   Kelly Reward Board.

April 1881–April 1883   Royal Commission on the Police Force of Victoria.

Note on weights, measures and money

To prevent anachronisms, the imperial system of weights and measures has been used throughout. Approximate equivalents are as follows:

Length   Mass
1 foot 30.5 cm   1 pound = 454 g
1 yard 0.914 m 1 stone = 6.36 kg
1 mile 1.61 km

Area
1 acre = 0.405 ha

Currency
There were 12 pennies (d.) in 1 shilling (s.), and 20 shillings in 1 pound (£). When decimal currency was adopted in Australia in 1966, two dollars were equivalent to one pound.

PREFACE

It has been twenty-two years since the publication of this book's first edition, *Ned Kelly in Popular Tradition*. In that time Australia has experienced significant cultural, social and economic change. Yet the image of our favourite hero/villain has not only persisted but has continued to grow, so much so that Ned Kelly was one of the national icons we displayed to the world at the 2000 Sydney Olympic Games. Despite this global projection of the bushranger's image Australians remain as ambivalent as always about Ned Kelly. But whether we celebrate or denigrate him, love him or loathe him, Ned Kelly remains inextricably bound up with our sense of national identity.

It was that relationship and its significance that the original book attempted to track and explain. Subsequent events have shown that very little in the book needed amendment. Consequently, this new, retitled edition takes the legend of Ned Kelly, folk hero, media hero and national hero, up to the present with a new concluding chapter and an updated bibliography. The text of the original book remains substantially unaltered, apart from some slight updating. The main changes have been to the Jerilderie Letter, the original of which was not available in 1980. The reappearance of the original letter has allowed for a more accurate transcript to be reproduced here, though these amendments do not alter the substance, style and passion of this remarkable document in any way.

There have been significant changes to the illustrations and layout. One of the aims of the 1980 book was to present selections of the extensive iconography of Ned Kelly, including songsheets, postcards, advertisements, film posters as well as official and unofficial photographs and the like. Many of these have been retained, though recaptioned and repositioned to complement the text and provide an enhanced visual experience for the reader.

Graham Seal

CURTIN UNIVERSITY OF
TECHNOLOGY 2002

CHAPTER 1

INTRODUCTION

H ow has an Irish–Australian bank robber, horse-stealer and murderer become Australia's only national hero? A century and a quarter after Ned Kelly was hanged in Melbourne gaol why are we still singing, writing, and making films about him, still trying to excuse, celebrate, or debunk a figure that has become the only approximation of a defining image this diverse continent can manage after more than two hundred years?

The 'how' and the 'why' of Edward Kelly, bushranger and national hero, are the questions this book tries to answer. In search of an answer we will need to range through time and space, to Britain in the eighteenth century, the United States of America in the nineteenth, and Australia from almost the beginning of white settlement to the present. Ned Kelly's story is the timeless tale of the hero, the man who transcends the often brutal or mundane realities of his existence to become a symbol of something larger than himself.

To understand Ned Kelly's unique staying power in the Australian consciousness we will need to know about some of the important elements in the Kelly saga and its ongoing mythology. These elements are Ned Kelly himself, the oral outlaw tradition to which he was heir, and the popular media industry that has proliferated around his image. It was, and continues to be, the constant interaction of these basic elements that has transformed a murdering bush larrikin with extensive local support into an Australian hero. Without this particular alchemy Ned Kelly would not be known by anyone other than a few old-timers and local historians.

But perhaps the single most important 'cause of Kelly' has been the bushranger's embodiment of certain characteristics generally felt to be uniquely Australian. Most of the popular portrayals of Ned Kelly show him defying authority, in the shape of the Victorian police, and stubbornly refusing to 'lie down and take it'. He is also seen to be on the side of the poor and the underdog and, like all heroes before or since, he is 'game'. He fights bravely and dies bravely for what he believes. Even today Australians may still be heard to compliment someone who displays courage with the saying, 'as game as Ned Kelly', or, 'as game as the Kelly Gang'.

Of all the popular attitudes towards Ned Kelly, an especially persistent one is that the bushranger represents that most pervasive of Australian myths — the belief that the 'real' Australia, the Australia of independence and freedom, is 'out there', 'in the bush', or 'the north', anywhere but in the cities. In one of the most urbanised countries on earth our popular poets have sung the praises of the bush, the outback, and the men who challenged that unpitying vastness. 'Clancy of the Overflow' and 'The Man from Snowy River' are Australian heroes because they took on something bigger than themselves. They took on Australia, or at least Paterson's symbols of Australia. Ned Kelly may have taken on only the colony of Victoria, and he may have lost, but his prestige stemmed from the fight itself, not the outcome. And because his particular struggle was so readily perceived in terms of the poor small farmers and selectors versus the mainly urban, centralised forces of wealth and power, Ned Kelly became the epitome of the rural myth, the Australian legend incarnate. It is not without significance that the final conflagration at Glenrowan erupted from the bushrangers' attempt to wreck a train, the supreme tool and symbol of nineteenth-century civilisation and progress.[1]

In spite of his position on the front line between the old and the new Australia, Ned Kelly was an anachronism, almost a generation too late for the heyday of bushranging during the 1860s. Ben Hall, Thunderbolt, Morgan and the rest rode and robbed before the country was securely chained to the urban centres of power with links of telegraph and rail. It was the resurgence of bushranging after it had become a part of the romantic past that was another important factor in Ned Kelly's rise to prominence. Not only was he the 'last of the bushrangers', Ned Kelly was the last real rural hero.

One of the first indications of the Kelly gang's ability to attract popular interest and celebration was the publication in 1879 of a pamphlet called *The Kelly Gang, or The Outlaws of the Wombat Ranges*. Produced by the enterprising proprietors of the *Mansfield Guardian*, a local Kelly country newspaper, the booklet included a number of songs about the bushranger. One of these, now known as 'The Bold Kelly Gang', is a good example of the slyly subversive material being propagated at the time.[2]

In the next year, 1880, a melodrama about the bushrangers played to Melbourne audiences. The only surviving record of this play is this song, in much the same style as 'The Bold Kelly Gang':

WE'RE THE JOLLIEST LOT OF THIEVES

We are the Jolliest lot of thieves
You ever came across,
We help the Harts, the Byrnes and Steves,
Dan Kelly and Ned the Boss.

Chorus:
For we always are the jolliest lot of thieves
You ever came across,
We help, the Harts, the Byrnes and Steves,
Dan Kelly and Ned the Boss.

When we go out upon the tramp,
The traps we never cross,
In woody dells we pitch our camp
And hobble every horse.

We act as telegraphs, you know,
And on the strict Q.T.
To them all paragraphs we show
And supply their grub and tea.

We cut the wires upon the line
And play the very deuce,
We cheat the traps near every time,
And make them of no use.

We are well paid you need not doubt,
We get a splendid screw,
For dodging here and there about
With naught but ill to do.[3]

Songs like these were the precursors of Ned Kelly's later viability as a media hero. As soon as word of the Kellys flashed by telegraph beyond the backwaters of north-eastern Victoria, journalists, photographers, and playwrights began bending their skills towards making Ned and his friends saleable copy. One quick-thinking photographer even produced postcards of three members of the gang and sold them throughout Victoria. Since then, a large industry has developed around Ned Kelly, or his image, and deluged a seemingly insatiable public with a flood of books, articles, songs, poems, a musical and a number of feature films, one of them Australia's earliest. By the 1940s Clive Turnbull found it necessary to grace the growing Kelly industry with a slim bibliography of forty-two published works, titled *Kellyana*. This only included the main publications in the field and did not cover newspaper articles, films, or works that dealt only in part with Kelly. A similar work today would run to hundreds of entries and would still have to omit many titles.

There was also another, underground, tradition that grew up around the image of Ned Kelly. About 1879 a broadsheet of four Kelly songs was published in Hobart, Tasmania. Three of the songs were those already given to the world in *The Kelly Gang, or The Outlaws of the Wombat Ranges*, but the fourth was a new one called 'The Ballad of the Kelly Gang', soon to escape from the printed page into oral tradition where it would eventually become the best-known of all the Kelly songs. Plainly in total sympathy with the bushrangers, 'The Ballad of the Kelly Gang' treats the Kellys' exploits with mischievous humour and is still sung in various

ONE OF THE POSTCARDS SOLD IN VICTORIA DUR- ING THE KELLY GANG'S OUTLAWRY. THE RIDERS ARE ALLEGEDLY NED KELLY AND TWO OTHER MEMBERS OF THE GANG. (POLICE MUSEUM, MELBOURNE)

versions today. A persistent though unprovable tradition holds that Joe Byrne, a member of the gang reputed to have been 'a bit literary', wrote the words, which are usually sung to the tune of 'The Wearing of the Green'. The identity of the composer hardly matters; 'The Ballad of the Kelly Gang' is a good song, and one that has stood the test of a century of singers. Here is the song as it appeared on the 1879 broadsheet:

THE BALLAD OF THE KELLY GANG

Oh, Paddy dear, and did you hear the news that's going round,
On the head of bold Ned Kelly they've placed two thousand pounds
For Dan, Steve Hart, and Byrne, two thousand each they'll give,
But if the sum were double, sure the Kelly boys will live.

Tis sad to think such plucky hearts in crime should be employed,
But with great persecution they've all been much annoyed,
Revenge is sweet, but in the bush they can defy the law,
Such stickings up and plunderings Colonials never saw.

T'was in November, '78 the Kelly gang came down
Just after shooting Kennedy to famed Euroa Town;
Blood horses rode they all upon, revolvers in their hand,
They took the township by surprise, and gold was their demand.

Into the Bank, Ned Kelly walked and bail up he did say,
Unlock your safes, hand out your cash, be quick, do not delay;
Without a murmur they obeyed the robbers bald [*sic*] command
Two thousand pounds in notes and gold they gave into his hand.

Now hand out all your arms you have, the audacious robbers said,
And all your ammunition, or a bullet through your head.
Your wife and children, too, must come, and make them look alive.
Get into these conveyances, we'll take you for a drive.

They drove them to a station about five miles away,
Where twenty men already had been bailed up all the day.
A hawker also shared the fate, which everybody knows
And came in handy to the gang, supplying them with clothes.

1879 HOBART BROADSIDE

OF KELLY SONGS. (MITCHELL

LIBRARY, SYDNEY)

Tune—"Going to Ballarat."

A sergeant and three constables set out from Mansfield town,
Near the end of last October, for to hunt the Kelly's down;
So they travelled to the Wombat, and they thought it quite a lark,
And they camped upon the borders of a creek called "Stringy Bark."

They had grub and ammunition there to last them many a week,
And next morning two of them rode out, all to explore the creek;
Leaving M'Intyre behind them, at the camp to cook the grub,
And Lonigan to sweep the floor, and boss the washing tub.

It was shortly after breakfast Mac thought he heard a noise,
So, gun in hand, he sallied out, to try and find the cause;
But he never saw the Kellys planted safe behind a log,
So he slithered back to smoke and yarn, and wire into the prog.

But bold Kelly and his comrades thought they'd like a nearer look,
For being short of grub, they wished to interview the cook;
And of fire-arms and cartridges they found they had too few,
So they longed to grab the pistols, guns, and ammunition too.

Both the bobbies, at a stump alone, they were then pleased to see,
A-watching of the billy boiling for the troopers' tea;
There they smoked and chatted gaily, never thinking of alarms,
Till they heard the fearful cry behind, "Bail up! throw up your arms."

The traps they started wildly, and Mac then firmly stood,
And threw up his arms, while Lonigan made tracks to gain the wood;
Reaching round for his revolver, but before he touched the stock,
Ned drew his trigger, and dropped him like a cock.

Then, after searching M'Intyre, all through the camp they went
And cleared the guns and cartridges and pistols from the tent,
But brave Kelly muttered sadly as he loaded up his gun,
"Oh, what a——pity the——tried to run!"

They rode into Jerilderie Town at 12 o'clock at night,
They roused the troopers from their beds, who were in dreadful fright.
And took them in their night shirts, ashamed I am to tell,
They cover them with revolvers, and locked them in a cell.

They next acquaint the women folks, that they intend to stay,
And take possession of the camp until the following day,
They fed their horses in the stalls, without the slightest fear,
And go and rest their weary limbs till daylight does appear.

Next morning being Sunday, of course they must be good,
They dress themselves in troopers clothes and Ned he chopped some wood
No one there suspecting them for troopers, and all, they pass,
And Dan, the most religious, took the trooper's wife to mass.

They spent the day most pleasantly, had plenty of good cheer,
Beef steaks and chops, tomato sauce, and several pints of beer;
The ladies in attendance indulged in pleasant talk,
And just to ease the troopers minds, they took them for a walk.

On Monday morning early, the master of the ground,
They took their horses to the forge, and had them shod all round,
They back were brought and mounted, their plans all laid so well,
In company with the troopers they stuck up Cox's hotel.

They bailed up all the servants and placed them in a room,
Saying do as we command you, or death will be your doom,
The Chinaman cook, so savy, cried, not knowing what to fear,
But they brought him to his senses with a lift under the ear.

All who had approached the house just shared a similar fate,
In a very short time the number was nearly twenty-eight.
They shouted freely for all hands and paid for what they drank,
And two of them remained in charge and two went to the bank.

The force was here repeated, that I've already told,
They bailed up all the bankers's clerks and robbed them of their gold
The manager could not be found, and Kelly in great wrath
Searched high and low, and luckily found him in his bath.

They destroyed communication, by telegraph at least,
Of threatening and of robbery they had a perfect feast,
Where they've gone's a mystery, and coppers cannot tell
Until we hear from them again I bid you all farewell.

SONGS OF THE KELLY GANG.

OH, Paddy dear, and did you hear the news that's going round,
On the head of bold Ned Kelly they've placed two thousand pounds
For Dan, Steve Hart, and Byrne, two thousand each they'll give,
But if the sum was double, sure the Kelly boys will live.

'Tis sad to think such plucky hearts in crime should be employed,
But with great persecution they've all been much annoyed,
Revenge is sweet, but in the bush they can defy the law,
Such stickings up and plunderings Colonials never saw.

'Twas in November, '78 the Kelly gang came down
Just after shooting Kennedy to famed Euroa Town;
Blood horses rode they all upon, revolvers in their hand,
They took the township by surprise, and gold was their demand.

Into the Bank, Ned Kelly walked, and bail up he did say,
Unlock your safe, hand out your cash, be quick, do not delay;
Without a murmur they obeyed, the robbers held command,
Two thousand pounds in notes and gold they gave into his hand.

Now hand out all the arms you have, the audacious robbers said,
And all your ammunition, or a bullet through your head.
Your wife and children, too, must come, and make them look alive,
Get into these conveyances, we'll take you for a drive.

They drove them to a station about five miles away,
Where twenty men already had been boiled up all the day,
A hawker also shared the fate, which everybody knows,
And came in handy to the gang, supplying them with clothes.

They next destroyed the telegraph by cutting down the wire
And of their left-off wearing clothes they made a bonfire,
Throughout the whole affair, my boys, they never fired a shot,
The way they worked was splendid and will never be forgot.

Oh, Paddy dear, do shed a tear, I can't but sympathise,
Those Kelly's are the devils, and they've made another rise.
This time across the Billybong Creek, on Morgan's ancient beat,
Where they robbed the Bank of thousands, and safely did retreat.

The matter may be serious, Pat, but sure I can't but laugh
To think the tales the Bobbys told should all amount to chaff;
They said they had them all hemmed in—they could not get away,
But they did turn up in New South Wales, and made their journey pay.

Tune 'Bold Sojer Boy.'

There's not a dodge worth knowing
Or showing, that's going,
But you'll learn (this isn't blowing)
From the bold Kelly Gang.

We have mates where'er we go
That, somehow, let us know
The approach of every foe
To the bold Kelly Gang.

There's not a peeler hiding
Wombat Ranges, hill or siding,
But would rather far be hiding,
Though he'd like to see us hung

We thin their ranks,
We rob the banks,
And say no thanks,
For what we do.
Oh, the terror of the camp,
Is the bold Kelly Gang.

Then if you want a spree,
Come with me, and you'll see
How grand it is to be,
In the bold Kelly Gang.

Sticking Up of the Euroa Bank.

So Kelly marched into the Bank,
A cheque all in his hand,
For to have it changed for money
Of Scott he did demand.

And when that he refused him,
He, looking at him straight,
Said 'See here, my name's Ned Kelly
And this here man's my mate.

With pistols pointed at his nut,
Poor Scott did stand amazed,
His stick he would have liked to cut,
But was with funk half crazed.

The poor cashier with real fear,
Stood trembling at the knees,
But at last they both seen twas no use
And handed out the keys.

The safe was quickly gutted then,
The drawers turned out as well,
The Kellys being quite polite,
Like any noble swell.

With flimsies, gold and silver coin,
The threepennies, and all,
Amounting to two thousand pounds
They made a glorious haul.

Sole Agent in Tasmania, for Kelly's Songs,
T. W. ALLEN,
17—ELIZABETH-STREET—17
HOBART TOWN.
AUTHOR of the "KELLY FAMILY," in Prose—
PRICE—SIXPENCE.

They next destroyed the telegraph by cutting down the wire
And of their left-off wearing clothes they made a small bonfire,
Throughout the whole affair, my boys, they never fired a shot,
The way they worked was splendid and will never be forgot.

Oh, Paddy dear, do shed a tear, I can't but sympathise,
Those Kelly's are the devils, and they've made another rise.
This time across the Billybong Creek, on Morgan's ancient beat,
Where they robbed the Bank of thousands, and safely did retreat.

The matter may be serious, Pat., but sure I can't but laugh,
To think the tales the Bobbys [*sic*] told should all amount to chaff;
'They said they had them all hemmed in—they could not get away,
But they did turn up in New South Wales, and made their journey pay.

They rode into Jerilderie town at 12 o'clock at night,
They roused the troopers from their beds who were in dreadful fright;
And took them in their nightshirts, ashamed I am to tell,
They covered them with revolvers, locked them in a cell.

They next acquaint the women folks that they intend to stay
And take possession of the camp until the following day.
They fed their horses in the stalls, without the slightest fear,
And go and rest their weary limbs till daylight does appear.

Next morning being Sunday, of course they must be good,
They dressed themselves in troopers' clothes and Ned he chopped
        some wood,
No one there suspected them, for troopers, and all, they pass,
And Dan, the most religious, took the trooper's wife to mass.

They spent the day most pleasantly, had plenty of good cheer,
Beefsteaks and chops, tomato sauce and several pints of beer.
The ladies in attendance indulged in pleasant talk,
And just to ease the troopers' mind, they took them for a walk.

On Monday morning early, the masters of the ground,
They took their horses to the forge, and had them shod all round.

Then back were brought and mounted, their plans all laid so well.
In company with the troopers they stick up Cox's Hotel.

They bailed up all the servants and placed them in a room,
Saying, 'Do as we command you, or death will be your doom',
The Chinaman cook, 'so savy', cried, not knowing what to fear,
But they brought him to his senses with a lift under the ear.

All who had approached the house just shared a similar fate,
In a very short time the number was nearly twenty-eight.
They shouted freely for all hands and paid for what they drank,
And two of them remained in charge and two went to the bank.

The force [*sic*] was here repeated, that I've already told,
They bailed up all the banker's clerks and robbed them of their gold.
The manager could not be found, and Kelly in great wrath
Searched high and low, and luckily found him in his bath.

They destroyed communication, by telegraph at least,
Of threatening and of robbery they had a perfect feast,
Where they've gone's a mystery, and coppers cannot tell
Until we hear from them again I bid you all farewell.[4]

Songs like this, together with a variety of Kelly beliefs, tales and forms of speech make up a strong oral tradition in Australian society. The particular items that form this tradition will be of interest to us later in the book. For the moment we need only to be aware of the existence of this folk tradition in the mouths and minds of white Australians who speak English as their first language. Kelly material of this type has been transmitted from person to person and from generation to generation by word of mouth. Some of the songs may have started their lives in printed form or become briefly transfixed upon pages at some stage of their existence. However, they and the other items in this sub-literary complex of belief have evolved primarily in the quicksilver state of oral communication and bear all the signs of adaptation and varia-tion that stamp them as authentically 'folk' — that is, as the formalised, unofficial and frequently subversive expressions of the common muse.

This folk tradition stands in contrast to the many literary, cinematic and other non-oral treatments of the Kelly story. The significant items and aspects of this 'media tradition', as I will call it throughout this book, will also interest us later on. Although the attitudes inherent in the media tradition were often drastically different to those of the oral folk tradition, both traditions have influenced each other over the last one hundred years. Each tradition has influenced the other at certain critical points to the extent where a regional bandit has become a defining, perhaps *the* defining, Australian persona. The combined effect of these two separate but mutually dependent interpretations of the Kelly story has been to create a popular tradition of great importance in comprehending certain attitudes and outlooks within Australian society.

Ned Kelly still provokes violent differences of opinion in this country. Discussion of the subject among a random selection of people is bound to polarise the group into two factions, those who consider Ned to be something not too far removed from a secular saint and those who insist that he was no more than a murderous thug. The interesting point about this, of course, is not so much whether one faction or another is right, but why an outlaw can inflame such feelings over a century after his death.

Good or bad, Ned Kelly is one of the few nationally and internationally identifiable symbols of Australia. He is certainly the only widely known historical figure that we have. There is a story, dating to at least World War I, of an English, an Irish and an Australian soldier, each of whom was intent on outraging the others' national pride. After the Pope had been duly insulted the King came in for his share of Australian humour. Stung by this affront, the English soldier blustered for a while in search of a suitably cutting rejoinder. The best he could come up with was, 'Well, we don't think much of Ned Kelly, either!'

The rest of this book traces the process through which Ned Kelly has come to occupy his present niche in the Australian consciousness. This will involve some historical detective work. It will also include the telling of Ned Kelly's story—as far as possible in the man's own words, and in the words of the people who saw him as something more than a common criminal.

CHAPTER 2

HIGHWAYMEN, OUTLAWS AND BUSHRANGERS

One of the most enduring aspects of Ned Kelly's image has been his role as a friend of the underdog, a living symbol of the vengeance of the inarticulate against those forces of law and power they believe to be oppressing them. This is the essential Ned Kelly, but surrounding this core are certain complementary characteristics that go to make up the bushranger's popular image. Take this song, for example:[1]

Ned Kelly was an Irishman, Kate Kelly she was bold,
They never robbed a poor man, but banks they robbed of gold.
It's come along my hearties and together we shall roam,
We'll make for yonder mountains, yon gullies or yon plains,
Before we'll work for government, bound down in iron chains.

This unusual piece concisely expresses the basic popular notions about Ned Kelly's image. If he was not actually born in Ireland he nevertheless retained strong emotional ties with the agonies of Irish nationalism, describing Victorian policemen, who were mostly Irish or of Irish descent, as cowards and traitors:

. . . who for a lazy loafing bilit left the ash corner, deserted the shamrock, the emblem of true wit and beauty to serve under a flag and a nation

11

that has destroyed massacreed [*sic*] and murdered their forefathers by the greatest of torture . . .[2]

Kate, one of Ned's four sisters, often appears in the Kelly pantheon in the role of heroine. Though her support for the bushrangers hardly extended to assisting them in bank robberies, such activities are portrayed as quite worthwhile in the song. To the Kellys and their sympathisers the banks were the symbols of all the things they detested — mortgages, the government, and the power of the wealthy landowners. 'Poor-man crushers' was how Ned Kelly would describe them. As a corollary of this attitude, the Kellys are said never to have robbed the poor; not because the poor weren't worth robbing but because, like the Kellys, they felt that they were suffering under a coercive administration and police force, both of which appeared to be working hand-in-glove with the larger Victorian landowners.

KATE KELLY, THE HEROINE.
(POLICE MUSEUM, MELBOURNE)

Finally, the song conveys ideas of physical freedom available in the wilderness, mountains and plains; the Australian equivalent of Robin Hood's 'merry greenwood'. Bound up with this is the more serious problem of political and social freedom from a power elite that is felt to be repressive.

Throughout the many expressions of popular sympathy with this image of Ned Kelly, the same sentiments occur again and again. From the earliest Kelly songs to the 'Smiling' Billy Blinkhorn composition of the 1930s, 'Poor Ned Kelly', the bushranger is portrayed as a symbol of resistance, even of retribution, against injustice and oppression. During his brief bushranging career of twenty months Ned Kelly was just such a symbol to his many sympathisers among the selectors and bush-workers of Victoria's north-eastern corner. And although his popular image ultimately transcended the status of local folk hero, it is this important initial stage of the Kelly legend that must be examined first.

In the years 1878 to 1880, Ned Kelly represented the final Australian flowering of a long tradition of popular bandit heroes, stretching back to the legendary Robin Hood and embracing the images of seventeenth- and eighteenth-century British highwaymen, American outlaws, and Ned Kelly's celebrated Australian predecessors, Jack Donahue, Ben Hall, and Frank Gardiner. The characteristics attributed to Ned Kelly in popular song and story have also been attributed to all of these historical figures and to many other bandit-heroes around the world. They therefore constitute a universal human reaction to perceived oppression, producing individuals who take their discontent past the point of muttered threats to the last resort of armed resistance — 'social bandits', as E. J. Hobsbawm has called such men?[3] To properly comprehend Ned Kelly's status as an Australian bandit and the consequent development of his image as a national symbol, we need to briefly trace this historical tradition.

The tradition of the 'noble robber' or the bold hero who robs the rich to benefit the poor can be found at least as early as the fourteenth century in Britain, when we begin to find mention of Robin Hood. Whether such an outlaw ever existed is of relatively little importance here. What matters is that Robin Hood became the archetypal figure of the British bandit tradition, and was credited with all the virtues of the noble robber through centuries of song, story and, more recently, Hollywood movies and television serials. These virtues, as expressed in the many Robin Hood ballads, were concisely stated by one of their most perceptive students, Francis J. Child:

> Robin Hood is a yeoman, outlawed for reasons not given but easily surmised. 'Courteous and free', religious in sentiment, and above all reverent of the Virgin, for the love of whom he is respectful to all women. He lives by the King's deer (though he loves no man in the world so much as his King) and by levies on the superfluity of the higher orders, secular and spiritual, bishops and archbishops, abbots,

bold barons and knights, but harms no husbandman or yeoman, and is friendly to poor men generally, imparting to them of what he takes from the rich. Courtesy, good temper, liberality and manliness are his chief marks; for courtesy and good temper he is a popular Gawain. Yeoman as he is, he has a kind of royal dignity, a princely grace, and a gentleman-like refinement of humour.[4]

So Robin Hood represents the beginnings of a coherent and continuous tradition of British outlaw heroes, figures portrayed in song as friends of the poor, usually driven to outlawry by some injustice. They are, however, brave, courteous to women, and use violence only when it is unavoidable or in justified revenge. Generally, they die bravely and usually through treachery. Such a set of ideal features only applies completely to the legendary Robin Hood, though the essential virtues of the poor man's friend and plunderer of the wealthy, together with the subsidiary attributes of bravery, courtesy to women and dying a 'game' death through treachery are also found clustered round the figures of certain British highwaymen.

These figures, the most famous being Dick Turpin and the Irish William Brennan, were described in the broadside ballads of their time as the direct successors to Robin Hood. One ballad printed as 'Turpin's Valour' has Turpin completely outwitting and robbing a wealthy, cheating lawyer, a judge, and a usurer impersonating a beggar. Turpin is the bold hero who humiliates the rich and the wealthy; finally he is betrayed and executed in the classical bandit style:

'I ventured bold at young and old,
And fairly fought them for their gold;
Of no mankind was I afraid,
But now, alas, I am betrayed.'[5]

Oral versions are much shorter than the original eighteen verses of this song and concentrate on Turpin's outwitting of the lawyer, like this one, usually known as 'Dick Turpin and the Lawyer' or 'Turpin Hero':

Turpin he was riding across Ramsey Moor,
Saw a lawyer a-riding before,

He said 'Old Gentleman don't you feel afraid
For to meet bold Turpin, the mischievous blade?'
With my hero, Turpin was a hero,
He was a valious Turpin-O.

Turpin said to the lawyer, 'Let us be so cute,
And put our money into our boot.'
'Oh no,' said the lawyer, 'I've made sure of mine,
For I've got it sewn in my coat cape behind.'
With my hero, etc.

So they rode till they came to the foot of the hill,
Turpin said to the lawyer, 'You must stand still,
For my horse is in want of a new saddle cloth,
And your coat cape it must come off.'
With my hero, etc.

'And when I have robbed you of all your store,
You know well where you can get more,
So at every town that you do come in,
You can tell them you've been robbed by the bold Turpin.'
With my hero, etc.

Turpin he was tried, in prison he was cast,
For shooting a gamecock hung at last,
Five hundred pounds that he laid by,
To pay Jack Ketch his salary high.
With my hero, etc.[6]

A song about Turpin's magical steed, 'Black Bess', contains these lines:

No poor man we robbed, nor did we oppress
The widows or orphans, my Bonny Black Bess.[7]

And much the same sentiments are found in a song about an earlier English highwayman, William Nevison (1639–84), or 'Swift Nicks'

as he was popularly known, because it was he who made the famous ride from London to York in one night, a feat usually attributed to Dick Turpin:

BOLD NEVISON

Did you ever hear tell of that hero,
Bold Nevison it was his name?
He rode about like a great hero,
And by that he gained a great fame.

He maintained himself like a gentleman,
Besides he was good to the poor;
He rode about like a bold hero,
And gained himself favour therefore.

Oh, the twenty-first day of the month
It proved an unfortunate day,
Captain Milton was riding to London,
And by mischance rode out of his way.

He called at a house by the roadside,
It was the sign of the Magpie,
Where Nevison he sat a-drinking,
And the Captain soon did him espy.

A constable soon then was sent for,
And a constable very soon came,
With three or four more in attendance,
With pistols charged in the King's name.

They demanded the name of this hero:
'My name it is Johnson', said he,
When the Captain laid hold of his shoulder,
Saying, 'Nevison, come thou with me.'

'Tis now before my lord the judge:
'Oh, guilty or not do you plead?'

He smiled at the judge and the jury,
And these were the words that he said:

'I have now robbed a gentleman of tuppence,
But I've never done murder nor killed.
But guilty I've been all my lifetime
So gentlemen do as you will.

Now when I rode on the highway
I always had money in store,
And whatever I took from the rich,
Why, I freely gave it to the poor.'[8]

Nevison and Turpin were popular bandit heroes in their day and long afterwards; versions of these and other songs about their adventures are still being recovered from oral tradition. Songs featuring the Irish highwaymen William Brennan and 'Captain' Grant are also quite frequently collected in Britain and America. These ballads present their heroes in much the same manner as their English counterparts, stressing the outlaw's bravery, courtesy, and his standing as a friend to the poor:

BRENNAN ON THE MOOR

It's of a fearless highwayman a story I will tell,
His name was William Brennan and in Ireland he did dwell,
And upon the Libbery Mountains he commenced his wild career
Where many a wealthy gentleman before him shook with fear.

Chorus:
  Bold and undaunted stood bold Brennan on the moor
  Brennan on the moor,
  Brennan on the moor
  Bold and undaunted stood Brennan on the moor.

A brace of loaded pistols he carried night and day,
He never robbed a poor man all on the King's highway,
But what he'd taken from the rich, like Turpin and Black Bess,
He always did divide between the widows in distress.

Brennan then robs a Pedlar Bawn of his watch and chain. But the pedlar soon robs it back again proving he 'was as good a man as he' and becoming a loyal accomplice of Brennan 'until his dying day'. With the aid of his wife, Brennan then robs the mayor of Cashel. Pursued by the authorities to the mountains, the outlaw receives nine wounds before yielding and, with his wife, is condemnded to death 'for robbing on the King's highway'.[9]

As well as the songs quoted here there are many other ballads about the exploits of British highwaymen, both famous and anonymous. Virtually all of them follow a similar pattern.[10] This was not just an invention of the songmakers. James Wright, an obscure highwayman executed at Tyburn in 1721, 'valued himself not a little that he had never injured any poor man'. 'Civil' Jack Turner, hanged six years later, was renowned for courtesy towards his victims, often returning a portion of what he had stolen from them.[11]

Some of the highwayman songs crossed the Atlantic to America in the mouths of sailors and immigrants, quite a few of them being still current in oral tradition. Building upon the basis of the imported British tradition, a number of indigenous bandit-heroes flourished in America in the wake of the Civil War. These outlaws were balladised in the same way as their British forerunners.

The best known of them was Jesse James (1847–82) who, according to his folklore, robbed the rich to benefit the poor, was unfailingly kind to women, orphans, and widows in distress, and was betrayed and gunned down by a member of his own gang after many years of notoriety. Jesse was a typical bandit figure who had the active support and sympathy of his own social group, the Kansas–Missouri dirt-farmers, most of whom were veterans of the defeated Confederate armies. When the Civil War ended, the State of Missouri refused to grant a full amnesty to ex-Confederate guerrillas and generally discriminated against them, instantly creating a cohesive social group that felt itself disadvantaged. To these people Jesse James was a marauding hero, avenging their sense of outrage and oppression. They fed him, clothed him, hid him and generally made it possible for him to survive as an outlaw for the extraordinarily long period of sixteen years. He was one of them, robbing only the banks and trains, never his own kind:

BALLAD OF JESSE JAMES

Jesse James was a lad who killed many a man;
He robbed the Glendale train.
He stole from the rich and he gave to the poor,
He'd a hand, a heart and a brain.

Chorus:
   Jesse had a wife to mourn for his life,
   Three children they were brave.
   But that dirty little coward that shot Mr Howard,
   Has laid Jesse James in his grave.

It was Robert Ford, that dirty little coward,
I wonder how he does feel;
For he ate Jesse's bread and he slept in Jesse's bed,
Then he laid Jesse James in his grave.

Jesse was a man, a friend to the poor,
He'd never see a man suffer pain;
And with his brother Frank he robbed the Chicago bank,
And he stopped the Glendale train.

It was on a Wednesday night, the moon was shining bright,
He stopped the Glendale train;
And the people all did say for many miles away,
It was robbed by Frank and Jesse James.

It was on a Saturday night, Jesse was at home,
Talking to his family brave;
Robert Ford came along like a thief in the night,
And laid Jesse James in his grave.

The people held their breath when they heard of Jesse's death,
And wondered how he ever came to die.
It was one of the gang called little Robert Ford,
That shot Jesse James on the sly.

Jesse went to his rest with a hand on his breast,
The Devil will be upon his knee;
He was born one day in the county of Shea,
And he came of a solitary race.

This song was made by Billy Gashade,
As soon as the news did arrive,
He said there was no man with the law in his hand,
Could take Jesse James alive.[12]

Other American badmen also managed to capitalise upon the sense of injustice prevalent during the same period, though mostly with less reason than Jesse. Billy the Kid, Sam Bass, and Quantrell, the Confederate guerrilla, all had songs made and sung about their real and imaginary doings in which they were characterised as friends of the poor and the scourge of the wealthy and unworthy.[13]

Over half a century later the dispossessed farmers of the Oklahoma dustbowl saw the gangster 'Pretty Boy' Floyd as an avenging angel of their despair and loss because he shot only policemen and robbed the banks that had called in the Okies' mortgages.[14]

This popular glorification of certain criminals according to a traditionally transmitted stereotype, and often with scant regard for the historical facts, indicates the existence of a channel through which discontent with certain aspects of society might flow in the absence or removal of any formal apparatus for political protest. Highwaymen or outlaw songs could also function as didactic texts for those amongst whom they circulated, emphasising certain attitudes and laying down rules for the appropriate behaviour of men placed outside the law for reasons not considered criminal by members of their own community. In other words, the highwayman tradition not only articulated discontent but also conditioned and restricted the behaviour of the bandit himself. In Britain, support for highwaymen may not have exceeded passive sympathy or romantic interest. But in America, and Australia, the same tradition informed the active discontent of social groups who felt themselves oppressed in some way, and also determined most of the actions of those outlaws and bushrangers who acted upon that discontent. In Australia, Ned Kelly was the paradigmatic figure of this tradition, though he was not the first.

It was inevitable that a penal colony would produce escapees, or 'bolters' as the early absconders were called. They existed, the lucky ones, by robbery and on handouts from their fellows who remained in servitude. Some were recaptured, most perished of exposure, loneliness, and insanity in the alien bush. The rest were picked off by Aboriginals. It is not recorded if any of them reached China, a sanctuary that many convicts believed to be just over the ranges. By 1805 these hopefuls were being described as 'bushrangers' and harsh Van Diemen's Land was full of them. Some were vicious and cruel, deranged by brutal treatment, though others were more restrained. Of these, the first to achieve prominence was Michael Howe, a colourful and resourceful man who styled himself 'Governor of the Ranges' and conducted negotiations with Lieutenant-Governor Thomas Davey, the 'Governor of the Town'. In 1816 one Thomas Seals reported an encounter with Howe's gang: 'They said that if I would be a friend to them, they would reward me well, and that there would be no danger in what they would give me for they were fully determined to be like Turpin to rob from the rich to give to the poor.'[15] Howe seems to have spent more time murdering treacherous companions and robbing the rich than in giving to the poor. But he knew that he was expected to behave in a proper highwayman fashion. When this proved difficult to accomplish he at least paid lip-service to the ideal.

Michael Howe was betrayed and killed in 1818. Six years later Mathew Brady continued the highwayman tradition, offering a reward for the then Lieutenant-Governor, Sir George Arthur:

> It has caused Mathew Brady much concern that such a person known as Sir George Arthur is at large. Twenty gallons of rum will be given to any person that will deliver his person unto me. I also caution John Priest that I will hang him for his ill-treatment of Mrs. Blackwell, at Newtown.[16]

The final sentence of this letter emphasises an important element of the Australian highwayman tradition that runs through the strategies of the most celebrated bushrangers — women must not be harmed in any way. Brady was fastidious in observing this rule and even went so far as to wound, beat and expel a gang member who molested a woman. Nevertheless Brady was eventually captured (by John Batman) and went to the gallows bravely, amidst much popular sympathy for his fate.

During the early 1840s another famous bushranger terrorised Van Diemen's Land. His name was Martin Cash and in company with Kavanagh and Jones he maintained the traditional respect for women. Cash also continued the preoccupation with grandiloquent letter-writing that would become a recurring feature in the careers of many bushrangers, culminating in Ned Kelly's defiant documents. The following letter was sent by Cash, Kavanagh and Jones to 'his Excellency the Governor':

> Messrs. Cash and Co. beg to notify his Excellency Sir John Franklin and his satellites that a very respectable person named Mrs. Cash is now falsely imprisoned in Hobart Town, and if the said Mrs. Cash is not released forthwith, and properly remunerated, we will, in the first instance, visit Government House and beginning with Sir John, administer a wholesome lesson in the shape of a sound flogging; after which we will pay the same currency to all his followers.
>
> Given under our hands, this day, at the residence of Mr. Kerr, of Dunrobin.[17]

Cash and Kavanagh were soon captured, tried, and sentenced to death. Their only defence was that they had killed and wounded for self-protection. The judge conceded this and their sentences were commuted to life on Norfolk Island. Kavanagh was soon hanged for participating in a mutiny, but Cash eventually earned a remission of his sentence and ended his days as an orchardist near Hobart.

Writing of bushrangers in general, James Bonwick, the historian of the Tasmanian variety, made this observation:

> . . . the bushranger was, in general, looked upon as a sort of martyr to convictism. It was he who had experienced the shame, the lash, the brutal taunt, from which they had suffered. It was he who rose against the tyranny of their prison despot and the dread consequences of their criminal law. He was the bold Robin Hood of their morning songs, and he was now the unfortunate victim of legal oppression, the captured

of the chase. Without denying the atrocities of his career, they would discover many extenuations for his crimes. His reckless daring would be the noblest chivalry; and the jovial freedom of his manners, the frankest generosity. His immoral jests would be cherished for posterity, and the eclat of his life and death would stimulate the worthy ambition of sympathising souls. The very gallows had a charm.[18]

Bonwick says that the convicts looked upon the bushranger as 'the bold Robin Hood of their morning songs'—this was certainly true of the first bushranger to be durably balladised, Jack Donahue. His exploits began in New South Wales during 1827 and were terminated three years later by police bullets in the scrub at Bringelly, near Sydney.

Sentenced to a lifetime of transportation in 1824–5 for intent to commit an unspecified felony, Donahue took to the bush within a few years of his arrival and had at least one song composed about his career, which was probably the basis for the famous 'Wild Colonial Boy'.[19] Donahue was credited by the ballads, and some witnesses, with most of the highwayman attributes: he was courteous to women (though these were in rather short supply in Sydney during the 1820s), never robbed the 'poor', who in this case were the convict and ex-convict population, was heroically daring, and died 'game'. He also had the sympathy and active support of his own social group — convicts, ex-convicts and ticket-of-leave men — who helped Donahue and his gang with information, supplies, and shelter.

BOLD JACK DONAHUE

There was a valiant highwayman of courage and renown,
Who scorned to live in slavery or humble to the Crown;
In Dublin city fair and free where first a breath he drew,
'Twas there they christened him the brave and bold Jack Donahue.

Chorus:
    Come all my hearties, we'll range the mountainside,
    Together we will plunder, together we will ride;
    We'll scour along the valleys and gallop o'er the plains,
    We scorn to live in slavery bound down with iron chains.

He scarce had been transported unto the Australian shore,
When he took to the highway as he had done before,
And every week in the newspaper was published something new,
Concerning all the valiant deeds of bold Jack Donahue.

As Donahue was cruising one summer afternoon,
Little was his notion that his death would be so soon;
When to his surprise the horse-police appeared to his view,
And in quick-time they did advance upon Jack Donahue.

The sergeant of the horse-police discharged his carabine,
And called aloud on Donahue to fight or to resign,
'I'd rather range these hills around like wolf or kangaroo,
Than work one hour for the government', cried bold Jack Donahue.

Six rounds he fought the horse-police until the fatal ball,
Which pierced his heart with cruel smart, caused Donahue to fall.
The sergeant and the corporal and all their cowardly crew,
It took them all their time to fall the bold Jack Donahue.

There were Freincy, Grant, bold Robin Hood, and Brennan and O'Hare,
But with Donahue the bushranger none of them could compare.
And now he's gone to heaven I hope, with the saints and angels, too,
May the Lord have mercy on the soul of bold Jack Donahue.[20]

Jack Donahue (or Dolan, Dooley, Dowling) is still remembered and celebrated in song today, not only in Australia but throughout the English-speaking world. Possibly more famous in their time, though now only faintly familiar, are the bushrangers of the 1860s, Frank Gardiner, Dan Morgan, Thunderbolt, and the tragic Ben Hall, to name only the most notorious.

To a greater or lesser extent, all these men consciously adhered to the now-established Australian highwayman tradition. Even such a pathetic and unbalanced character as Dan 'Mad Dog' Morgan, who operated on the New South Wales and Victorian border from 1863 to 1865, had some notion about the proper way for a bushranger to behave. Morgan often shouted farm workers to their bosses' grog and inquired whether they were receiving fair treatment. He was considerate to women and known as 'the travellers' friend'. There is in existence a set of lyrics about Morgan that bears the signs of a folk origin and transmission, casting its hero in the classic highwayman mould:

THE DEATH OF MORGAN

Throughout Australian History no tongue or pen can tell
Of such preconcerted treachery — there is no parallel —
As the tragic deed of Morgan's death; without warning he was shot
On Peechelba station, it will never be forgot.

I have oft-times heard of murders in Australia's golden land,
But such an open daylight scene of thirty in a band,
Assembled at the dawn of day, and then to separate,
Behind the trees, some on their knees, awaiting Morgan's fate.

Too busy was the servant-maid; she trotted half the night
From Macpherson's down to Rutherford's tidings to recite.
A messenger was sent away who for his neck had no regard,
He returned with a troop of traps in hopes of their reward.

But they were all disappointed; McQuinlan was the man
Who fired from his rifle and shot rebellious Dan
Concealed he stood behind a tree till his victim came in view,
And as Morgan passed his doom was cast — the unhappy man he slew.

There was a rush for trophies, soon as the man was dead;
They cut off his beard, his ears, and the hair from off his head.
In truth it was a hideous sight as he struggled on the ground,
They tore the clothes from off his back and exposed the fatal wound.

Oh, Morgan was the travellers' friend; the squatters all rejoice
That the outlaw's life is at an end, no more they'll hear his voice.
Success attend all highwaymen who do the poor some good;
But my curse attend a treacherous man who'd shed another's blood.

Farewell to Burke [*sic*], O'Meally, young Gilbert and Ben Hall,
Likewise to Daniel Morgan, who fell by rifle-ball;
So all young men be warned and never take up arms,
Remember this, how true it is, bushranging hath no charms![21]

A verse of what appears to be a traditional ballad about the New England bushranger 'Thunderbolt' (Frederick Ward — sometimes confused with Frederick Britten, his one-time accomplice) goes like this:

My name is Frederick Ward, I am a native of this isle;
I rob the rich to feed the poor and make the children smile.[22]

Although Thunderbolt has not developed a very strong folkloric presence outside his home territory there are numerous local traditions that reinforce the 'highwayman' characterisation of the bushranger given in the lines above. He is said to have been considerate to children and the sick, gallant toward women, and against violence of any sort. A very strong oral tradition has it that the 'Thunderbolt' shot dead by a policeman in 1870 was not Ward at all but his look-alike younger or half-brother. Different versions of this story have the real Thunderbolt escaping to South America or starting a new life in Western Australia. In a later chapter we will see how a similar belief in the survival of a popular hero became attached to the Kelly legend.

Another bandit of the troubled 1860s, Francis Christie, *alias* Clark *alias* Gardiner, known to his accomplices as 'Darkie', first attracted widespread public interest when he masterminded the Eugowra Rocks robbery of the Forbes Gold Escort in 1862. Accompanied by eleven others, Gardiner shot up the mail coach and the police guard in it and made off with almost £4000 in cash, and well over 2000 ounces of gold, together with the Royal Mail. Most of the loot was recovered quite soon after the robbery and Gardiner disappeared to Queensland with his mistress, Kitty Brown, Ben Hall's sister-in-law. Frank was eventually captured in 1864 through a careless letter from Kitty to her family in New South Wales.

Because he had not committed murder (as far as anyone knew) Gardiner was spared the gallows and given thirty-two years' hard labour

instead. After ten years of constant agitation by his family, Gardiner was released into exile in 1874 and put aboard a ship bound for Asia. He ended his days as a publican in San Francisco during the 1890s. Gardiner was aware that in order to retain the vital sympathy of the bush farmers and workers, he had to be seen to act in accordance with the conventions of the highwayman tradition already established through Jack Donahue's activities and his song. He even took the trouble to write to a newspaper that had accused him of acting in an unchivalrous manner during some of his robberies:

> It is said that I took the boots off a man's feet, and that I also took the last shillings that another man had, I wish it to be made known that I did not do anything of the kind. The man that took the boots was in my company, and for so doing I discharged him . . . Silver I never took from a man yet, and the shot that was fired at the sticking up of Messrs. Horsington and Hewitt was by accident and the man who did it I also discharged. As for a mean, low or petty action, I never committed it in my life.

Gardiner signed himself: 'Fearing nothing, I remain Prince of Toby-men, Francis Gardner [sic], the Highwayman.'[23]

In 1863 the editor of the Sydney Morning Herald complained that some people saw Gardiner and his accomplices as: '. . . avengers of the poor and only the robbers of the rich.'[24] This was exactly the image that Gardiner and his more intelligent companions needed to culti-vate in order to stay alive. When a one-time crony of Gardiner's mur-dered a local Abercrombie (NSW) farmer in a drunken brawl, his previously loyal supporters were quick to react. Johnny Piesley had enjoyed extensive local popularity and aid, by which he continually eluded the police. After the murder he lost this support and was forced to leave the district to avoid capture. He was arrested within a few weeks of vacating his home territory. It is hardly surprising that there are no songs about Piesley, who showed himself to be incapable of adhering to the moral requirements of the highwayman tradition, while Frank Gardiner, who went to some lengths to foster the appropriate image, is called 'the poor man's friend' in his song.

FRANK GARDINER

Frank Gardiner he is caught at last; he lies in Sydney gaol,
For wounding Sergeant Middleton and robbing the Mudgee Mail,
For plundering of the gold escort, the Cargo Mail also;
And it was for gold he made so bold, and not so long ago.

His daring deeds surprised them all throughout the Sydney land,
And on his friends he gave a call and quickly raised a band.
And fortune always favoured him until the time of late,
When Bourke and poor O'Meally too met with their dreadful fates.

Young Vane he surrendered, Ben Hall he got some wounds,
As for Johnny Gilbert, at Binalong was found;
Alone he was, he lost his horse, three troopers hove in sight,
He fought the three most manfully, got slaughtered in the fight.

When lives you take, a warning, boys, a woman never trust;
She will turn round, I will be bound, Queen's evidence the first.
Two and thirty years he's doomed to slave all for the Crown,
And well may he say he cursed the day he met Old Mother Brown.

Day after day they remanded him, escorted to the bar;
Fresh charges brought against him from neighbours near and far.
But now it is all over, his sentence is brought down,
He's doing two and thirty years, he's doomed to serve the Crown.

Farewell, adieu to outlawed Frank, he was the poor man's friend;
The government has secured him, the laws he did offend.
He boldly stood his trial and answered in a breath;
'Do what you will, you can but kill, I have no fear of death.'[25]

Even more than Gardiner, Ben Hall was widely balladised as the
friend of the poor, driven to bushranging by official persecution. Hall
was the well-respected owner of a cattle station at Breeza, near Forbes,
New South Wales. He was arrested in 1862 for being present while Frank
Gardiner, whom Hall knew well, bailed up a passing teamster. After a

month in gaol, Hall was acquitted. He returned to find his wife had deserted him, taking their baby son with her. Deeply upset by this, Hall fell in with Gardiner's gang.

Twelve days after the Eugowra Rocks holdup Hall was arrested on suspicion of armed robbery. He was released two months later when an informer failed to implicate him as a member of the gang. Once again Hall returned home to disaster, this time financial. While he was in gaol the police had burned his house and left his cattle to die, penned in the mustering yard. Six months later the police found Hall in the company of Patsy Daley, a local wild boy wanted for armed robbery and bailing up a police station. Knowing that in the eyes of the law he was an accomplice to Daley's crimes, Ben Hall galloped into the bush and into the beginning of his legend as a tragic figure, hounded to outlawry by the unjust forces of law and order. There are a number of powerful traditional ballads about Ben Hall; this is the one that perhaps expresses the depth of popular feeling about the bushranger most effectively:

BOLD BEN HALL

Come all Australian sons to me, a hero has been slain,
And cowardly butchered in his sleep upon the Lachlan Plain.
Oh, do not stay your seemly grief, but let a teardrop fall,
Oh, so many hearts will always mourn the fate of bold Ben Hall.

No brand of Cain ever stamped his brow, no widow's curse did fall;
When times were bad the squatters dread the name of bold Ben Hall.
He never robbed a needy chap, his records best will show,
He was staunch and loyal to his friends and manly to the foe.

Oh, and savagely they murdered him, those cowardly blue-coat imps,
Who were set on to where he slept by informing peelers' pimps,
Ever since the good old days of Turpin and Duval,
The people's friends were outlaws too, and so was bold Ben Hall.[26]

Ben Hall was killed in 1865, his body riddled with police bullets. By the end of the 1860s all the famous bushrangers had been shot, hanged, or gaoled and the country settled down to a relatively peaceful period of expansion and prosperity. By the mid-1870s bushrangers were already spoken of in some quarters as part of a romantic past. But then in 1878, a group of bush larrikins gunned down three policemen in the dark Wombat Ranges of north-eastern Victoria, beside a creek called Stringybark. The final and most enduring Australian manifestation of the highwayman tradition was a tall, strong, bearded man in his early twenties, who described the Victorian police as:

> . . . a parcel of big ugly fat necked wombat headed big bellied magpie legged narrow hipped splaw-footed sons of Irish Bailiffs or english landlords which is better known as Officers of Justice or Victorian Police who some calls honest gentlemen . . . [27]

This, and the rest of the Jerilderie Letter, leaves little doubt that Ned Kelly and his friends had no time for policemen, or for the law in general. To uncover the motivations behind such remarkable invective we need to go back some years before those words were committed to paper.

CHAPTER 3

'FEARLESS, FREE AND BOLD'

he Kelly family and their numerous relatives formed an extensive system of clan-like interdependence based upon their common Irish heritage and their uneasy relationship with the forces of law and order. Ned Kelly's father, John, or 'Red', Kelly was transported to Van Diemen's Land (Tasmania) in 1841 for stealing two pigs in his native Tipperary, where he had been employed as a gamekeeper. By 1848 he had served out his seven years' sentence and was freed, aged twenty-nine. Apart from a fine for being drunk and disorderly and an incident of trespassing on a free man's potato patch, 'Red' Kelly had been a very well-behaved convict.

By 1850 'Red' had met and married Ellen, daughter of James Quinn, originally an Irish 'bounty' immigrant, but then living in Wallan Wallan, Victoria. After a number of relocations and incidents with the law, both the Kelly and the Quinn families settled in the same general area during the 1860s; the Quinns at Glenmore station on the King River, and the Kellys near Greta. By this time, 1867, 'Red' Kelly had been dead for six months and Ned, at twelve years of age, was the head of the Kelly household which, including his mother and himself, numbered nine, the children ranging in age from two to fourteen.

Contact between the Kellys and Quinns remained close throughout the 1850s and 1860s. Two of Ellen Kelly's sisters, Kate and Jane, had

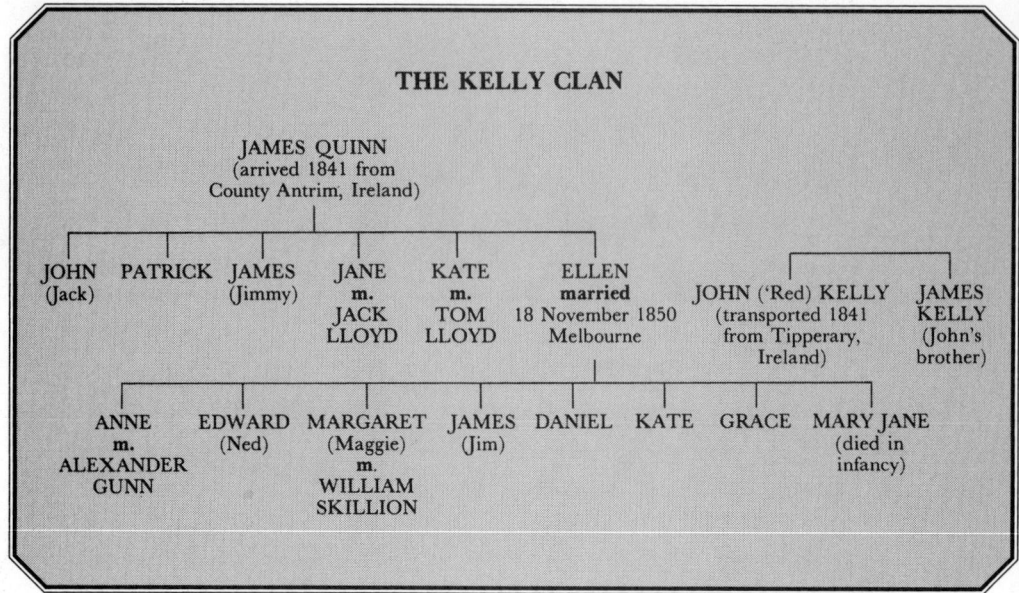

THE KELLY CLAN

JAMES QUINN
(arrived 1841 from
County Antrim, Ireland)

JOHN PATRICK JAMES   JANE   KATE   ELLEN   JOHN ('Red) KELLY   JAMES
(Jack)   (Jimmy) m.   m.   married   (transported 1841   KELLY
                        JACK   TOM   18 November 1850 from Tipperary,   (John's
                        LLOYD   LLOYD   Melbourne   Ireland)   brother)

     ANNE   EDWARD   MARGARET   JAMES   DANIEL   KATE   GRACE   MARY JANE
     m.   (Ned)   (Maggie)   (Jim)   (died in
ALEXANDER   m.   infancy)
   GUNN   WILLIAM
                        SKILLION

married two brothers, Jack and Tom Lloyd, during the 1850s and both
were now living near Greta. Through these marriages the Lloyd family
also became part of the extensive network of family and friends who
were to provide the basis of the Kelly gang's 'bush telegraph' system
between 1878 and 1880.

It was in the Greta district that Ned Kelly first collided with the law
at the age of fourteen. A Chinaman claimed that Ned had beaten him
with a stick, shouting: 'I'm a bushranger. Give up your money or I'll
beat you to death.' Whatever the truth behind this slightly bizarre incident, Ned was discharged after a number of remands and the presentation of an extremely dubious case by the police.

The next year, Ned was in trouble again. Charged with aiding the
bushranger Harry Power in some of his robberies, he was eventually
freed for lack of evidence, though he spent almost two months in gaol.
A few weeks before Ned's release, Power was captured by a party of police
who were led to the bushranger's hiding place (now Power's Lookout)
by an informer named 'L', probably Jack Lloyd. This was the price of
keeping Ned out of gaol.[1] Such an act of treachery by Power's former
supporters was made possible by Power's own neglect of the bushranger's
ethic. He robbed the only squatter in the district who was respected
by the Lloyds, Kellys, and Quinns, one Robert McBean, a seemingly
fair-minded man who paid good wages and whose wife had once
released impounded stock to the Lloyd family.

So Ned got off again. He was not so fortunate later that year though,
being sentenced to six months' hard labour in Beechworth gaol con-

victed of assault and indecent behaviour. Three weeks after serving out four months of this sentence (two months off for good behaviour), he was arrested on a charge of horse-theft, convicted of receiving a stolen horse and sent down for three years' hard labour, most of which he would do in Melbourne's Pentridge gaol.

While the young Ned Kelly was getting himself in and out of trouble, other members of the Kelly, Quinn, and Lloyd clan were making their names and activities familiar to the local police. Charges of stock-duffing and brawling were most frequently laid against Ned's relatives, with varying degrees of success. Often their cases were discharged for lack of evidence, though when the police finally did manage to make a charge stick, the offenders were sent to prison for long periods. John Lloyd sen. and Thomas Lloyd sen. had not long finished a five-year term apiece for cattle stealing when Ned was sent to Pentridge. Patrick Quinn was doing four years for grievous bodily harm, and Ned's uncle, James Kelly sen., was serving fifteen years for arson, a commutation of the original death penalty. James Kelly jun., Ned's younger brother, was soon to collect a five-year sentence for cattle stealing, and John Lloyd sen. forfeited another four years of his life for maliciously killing a horse in 1873.

However, the Kellys, Ned at least, also found time for some legal and even constructive activities. In his very young days Ned Kelly had saved a child from drowning, and later became the unofficial bare-knuckle boxing champion of the district when he thrashed the formidable Isaiah 'Wild' Wright in a gruelling twenty-round bout.

After his release from Pentridge in February 1874, Ned broke away from the seemingly inevitable pattern of arrest, conviction, and imprisonment, and worked steadily as a bush labourer around north-eastern Victoria and in the Riverina. In 1877 he was fined for being drunk and disorderly after a fight with four policemen, two of whom, Constables Fitzpatrick and Lonigan, were to play further roles in the Kelly tragedy. Other than this he appeared to be leading a blameless life. 'Appeared' seems to be the appropriate word. From late 1876 Ned and his stepfather, George King (an American prospector who married Ellen Kelly in 1874), were probably engaged in a large-scale duffing operation in the King Valley and surrounding districts. They were never caught, though they may well have been if Ned Kelly's elevation to murderer and outlaw had not transcended such relatively minor infractions of the law.

Between 1856 and 1880 the police records show a total of seventy-two arrests of three Quinns, four Lloyds and six Kellys.[2] Apart from the murders at Stringybark Creek, most of these charges were for stock-stealing or related offences, and for various forms of physical violence ranging from assault on police officers to manslaughter. Of these charges, forty-one were dismissed by the courts, generally for lack of evidence. This significant dismissal rate inevitably raises questions about the attitude of the police force towards the Kellys and their friends. Indeed, the same questions were being asked at the time, not only by the Kellys but by many other farmers and selectors in north-eastern Victoria, a substantial number of whom felt that they were being disadvantaged by a combination of police, local authorities, and the larger landowners.[3] An outline of the economy and administration of the area during this period is clearly important for understanding why the Kellys acted as they did.

Historians have pointed out that although land settlement was important in Australia during the 1870s, the decisive developments were the growth of manufacturing industries in the cities so that business and administration were centralised in the colonial capitals. This, in Victoria, together with the influence of the railways in transforming many rural areas from a grazing to a farming economy, resulted in the economic success of people with farming skills, some capital, and reasonably fertile land close to the railways. Many people, like the Kellys

THE KELLY COUNTRY.

(FROM *NED KELLY IN PICTURES*,

SOUTHDOWN PRESS, N.D.)

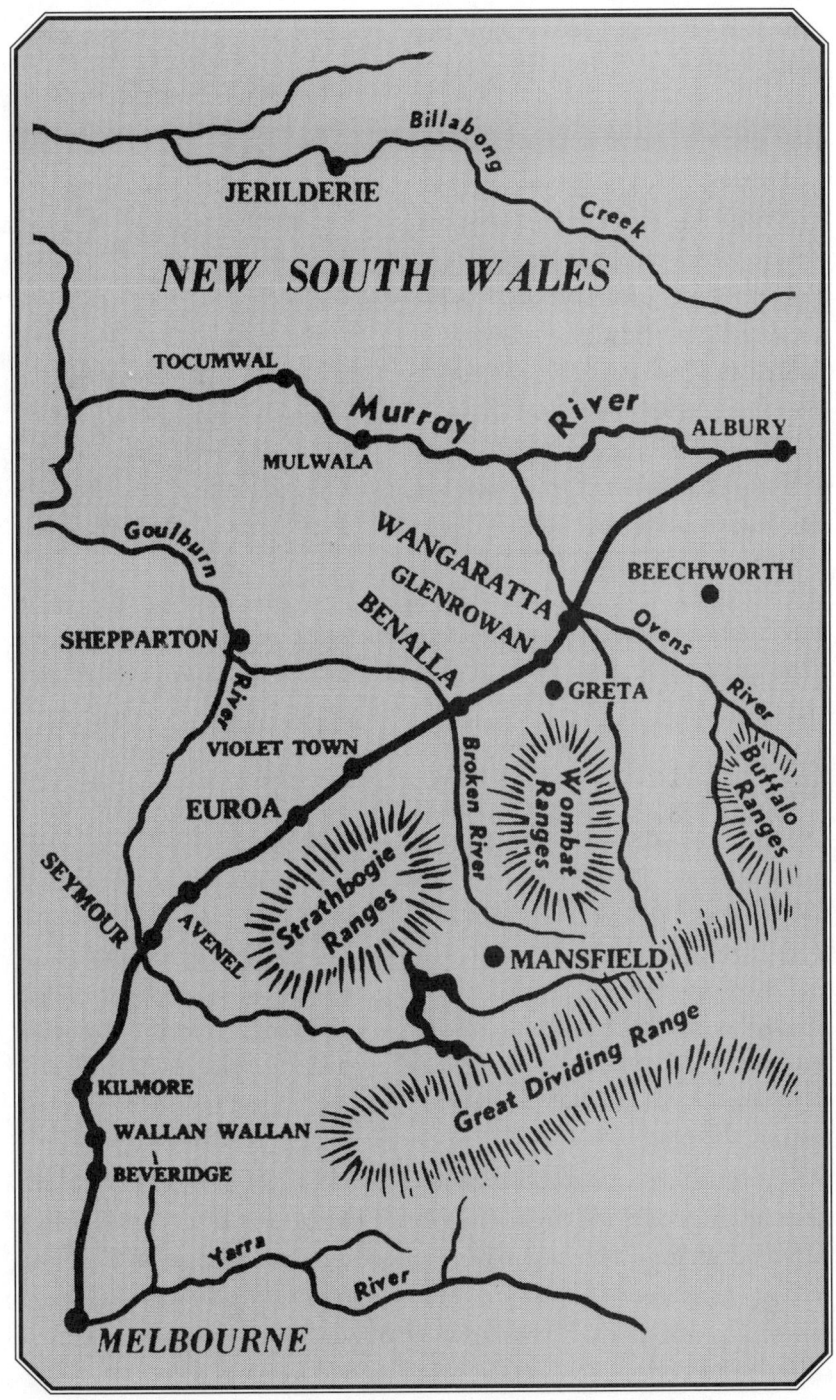

NED KELLY: THE
EX-CONVICT. (POLICE
MUSEUM, MELBOURNE)

and their relations, lacking these req-
uisites were unable to participate in
this shift of economic emphasis and
so were deprived of its benefits.[4]

During the same period, the increasing centralisation of administration widened the existing gap in
co-ordination and comprehension
between police headquarters in Melbourne and the practical problems of
the local constabulary. In 1854–56,
the Victoria Police in Melbourne
were reorganised on the model of
the London Metropolitan Police.[5]
This was a reasonably satisfactory sys-
tem for the rapidly expanding capital, but was not geared to handle
the policing of rural areas like the north-eastern district, where a system similar to that of the New South Wales trooper police was used.
Structured after the militaristic Royal Irish Constabulary, the Victorian
version was no more popular than its predecessor across the border.[6]
Nevertheless, the organisation and manning of the Victoria Police contributed to the inefficiency of the force and the general disdain in which
it was held in many quarters. Police administration of country districts was constantly hampered by changes of personnel that resulted
in the removal of men familiar with the local terrain and population
and their replacement by those lacking the experience and knowledge
needed to handle the often refractory locals. This certainly appears to
have been the case in the north-eastern district, which was a region
notorious for stock-theft for at least thirty years before the Kelly outbreak.[7]

The problems of local policing were compounded by the crippling
necessity to consult a higher authority before any significant action
could be taken and having to requisition and document even the most
trifling items. Horses, housing, and men were all inadequate and there
was strong antipathy between senior officers. As the Royal Commission on the Police Force of Victoria finally stated in 1881:

. . . immediately prior to the Kelly outbreak, and for some time previously, the administration of the police in the north-eastern district
was not satisfactory, either as regards the number and distribution of
the constabulary or the manner in which they were armed and mounted;
and that a grave error was committed in abolishing the police station
at Glenmore, and in reducing the strength of the stations at Stanley,
Yackandandah, Tallangatta, El Dorado and Beechworth.[8]

Such short-comings of the Victorian police contributed to the
generally poor image of the force.[9] In addition the small selectors of
the north-eastern district generally believed the police to be on the
side of the squatters, the banks, and shopkeepers.[10] This belief inflamed
the strong feelings that already existed in the area, the endemic stock-
stealing being a way of evening the score with the squatters for their
apparent collusion with the police in impounding stray beasts. To regain
an impounded horse or cow it was necessary to pay a fine to the im-
pounder. This practice is one of the major grievances expressed in Ned
Kelly's Cameron and Jerilderie Letters.

At the Victorian Crown Lands Commission of 1878–79, evidence
was given that selectors often had no means of physical survival other
than stealing from the larger squatters, and that this practice was not
only common but also viewed by struggling selectors as the accepted
procedure.[11] The witness, Charles Barbour, a prominent wealthy land-
owner,[12] was also of the opinion that there were some 'fine honourable
men' amongst these stock-duffing free-selectors.

The attitudes described by Barbour were typical of the rural labour-
ing classes in the nineteenth century. Many small selectors considered
the law allowing some men to impound stock was nothing more than
legalised duffing, and that their own stock-stealing was certainly no
more reprehensible.

Linked with this sort of grievance was the injustice that the Quinns,
Kellys, and Lloyds reportedly felt about their difficulty in obtaining
Crown land for selection. Behind the specially closed doors of the Royal
Commission, William B. Montford, Sergeant of Police in the north-
eastern district from 1858 to 1867, gave his version of the cause of the
outbreak and what measures might have averted it, based upon his
experience and knowledge of the Kellys and their associates:

... a great deal of the difficulty with these men [selectors like the Quinns and Kellys] would be got over if they felt they were treated with equal justice — that there was no 'down' upon them. They are much more tractable if they feel that they are treated with equal justice. As to the refusal of land to suspected persons (harbourers) . . . the Crown Lands Department should work in concert with the police — to place me in a position that I can use the provision of the Land Act as a lever to influence the applicants for land in the north-eastern district . . . I find from conversation with some of these men that if they recognised me — that is the head of the police force there — as the arbiter of their destinies to a certain extent, with regard to the taking and selling of Crown Lands — in other words, that it would depend on their good behaviour — by that, a lever would be put in our hands which would have more potency than any army of police. The result, I think would be that it would prevent them from harbouring criminals and would give them a direct incentive to place themselves on good terms with the police, whereas at the present time, they have no such feeling. Their whole object is to obtain land and if their individual interests depended upon their good behaviour among the population where they are, it would be half the battle towards making good citizens of them.[13]

Sergeant Montford, obviously not used to expressing such thoughts to his superiors, has been quoted at length here to illustrate some basic grievances of the Kellys and their sympathisers, and also to show the sort of local understanding that even a policeman could, in time, attain.[14] Rural discontent about the equity of the selection system was not restricted to the north-eastern district. The Victorian Crown Lands Commission was one response to the general dissatisfaction.[15] The actions of the Kellys and their sympathisers were a very different response to the same fundamental problems.

Why was it the Kellys who took up arms, and not one of the many similar families of selectors and bush workers who drank, duffed, and brawled across north-eastern Victoria? That question is difficult to answer; certainly the stage was set for trouble between the Kellys and the police. In 1877 Superintendent Nicolson reported the results of an official visit he had paid to the Kelly home:

. . . until the gang referred to [the Kellys and their relations] is rooted out of the neighbourhood one of the most experienced and successful mounted constables in the district will be required in charge of Greta . . . Without oppressing the people or worrying them in any way you should endeavour, whenever they commit any paltry crime, to bring them to Pentridge. Even on a paltry sentence.[16]

This makes it clear that the Kellys, Quinns, and Lloyds were the objects of serious and prolonged police concern and surveillance.[17] And we already know what Ned Kelly thought of the Victorian police.

But something more was necessary to set the stage alight. As is often the case, the spark that ignited the Kelly explosion began as a rather trivial incident involving the Kellys and a blundering Irish policeman.

CHAPTER

—4—

'WHAT A BLOODY PITY THE BASTARD TRIED TO RUN'

I n March of 1878, Constable Fitzpatrick was sent to take charge of the Greta police station for a few days. He had seen a police notice of the issue of a warrant for Dan Kelly in relation to a case of horse-stealing. After refreshing himself at one hotel, at least, Fitzpatrick decided, against orders, to bring in Dan Kelly. He rode off towards Greta with no warrant for Dan's arrest and no ability for the job either — he was later dismissed from the force for being untrustworthy and negligent in the performance of his duty.

When he was heard from again, Fitzpatrick said that he had tried to arrest Dan but was attacked by Mrs Kelly, Dan, Bill Skillion (husband of Margaret Kelly) and 'Bricky' Williamson — and that he had been shot in the wrist by Ned Kelly himself.[1]

The Kellys' version was that Fitzpatrick had arrived drunk, attempted to molest one of the Kelly girls, and generally insulted and bullied those present. Yes, there was a struggle during which Fitzpatrick shot himself in the wrist, but Ned had not even been there. It seems likely that no one was telling the truth. Ned Kelly probably was present but he probably did not shoot Fitzpatrick. Whatever actually took place that day in Greta, the outcome was the arrest of Skillion, Willliamson and Mrs Kelly, and a £100 reward for the capture of Ned Kelly. At the trial Mrs Kelly was given the unusually severe sentence of three years in Pentridge solely on Fitzpatrick's questionable evidence. Williamson and Skillion received six years apiece.

This sentence was one of the earliest components of the Kellys' image as the victims of official persecution and injustice. Popular opinion in the north-eastern district at the time held Fitzpatrick in contempt as a liar while the Kellys were seen as the victims of police harassment.[2] The same sentiment finds an outlet in one of the Kelly ballads, 'Kelly Was Their Captain':

Now Kennedy, Scanlon and Lonigan in death were lying low,
When Ned amongst them recognised his old and vitreous [sic] foe;
Then thoughts came of his mother with a baby at her breast,
And it filled Ned's heart with anger, and the country knows the rest.

From the time of their mother's arrest Ned and Dan stuck to the bush, rocking a gold cradle and nursing their anger at this ultimate proof of police tyranny. About 5 p.m. on 26 October, together with Steve Hart, Joe Byrne and Tom Lloyd jun.,[3] they came upon the camp of Constables Scanlon and Lonigan who, together with Constable McIntyre and Sergeant Kennedy, were searching for the Kellys along the banks of Stringybark Creek, high in the Wombat Ranges.

The Kellys called on the two policemen to 'Bail up!' McIntyre obeyed but Lonigan grabbed his pistol and ran for cover. As he raised his head above a sheltering log to fire at the bushrangers, Ned Kelly shot him dead.

An hour or so later, Sergeant Kennedy and Constable Scanlon returned to the camp. McIntyre, assured that the bushrangers would let him and the others live if they surrendered, told the two riders that they were surrounded. Ned Kelly then revealed himself and shouted 'Bail up!' Scanlon got off one shot before a bullet from Ned's rifle killed him. Kennedy slid off his mount and made for the bush. McIntyre, seizing the opportunity of the moment, vaulted onto the sergeant's horse and escaped.[4] A short gun battle between Kennedy and the Kelly brothers ended with the policeman being fatally wounded by Ned. Believing that the policeman could not live, Ned administered a *coup de grâce* and covered the body with the sergeant's own cloak.

Constable McIntyre brought the shocking news to Mansfield the following afternoon. In his fear he had turned Kennedy's horse loose and hidden in the bush. When details of the murders reached Melbourne the public reacted with revulsion, encouraging the Berry govern-

ment to rush an adaptation of the New South Wales Felons
Apprehension Act through the Victorian Parliament.
This legislation, a throwback to the bushranging heyday
of the 1860s, the earlier penal years, and even further back
to the medieval institution of outlawry, was essentially a means of impos-
ing what amounted to martial law on any given area. Under the Act,
those proclaimed as outlaws could be shot on sight by anyone at all.
Persons suspected of harbouring or aiding outlaws could be arrested
and presumed guilty on the unsupported allegation of another person.
The maximum sentence for this offence was fifteen years' hard labour.
Any Justice of the Peace or police officer was empowered to enter and
search premises without a warrant if he suspected outlaws were being
harboured there. Finally, the police were able to commandeer horses,
arms, or supplies when in pursuit of outlaws, the amount of compen-
sation for such requisitions being decided by the government.[5]

The Victorian Felons Apprehension Act became effective on 12 November 1878. From that day north-eastern Victoria became an occupied
province. Police had the power of arbitrary arrest and imprisonment;
individuals and homes were under continuous surveillance and were
frequently made the objects of misguided police raids and searches.
Parties of armed police constantly patrolled the district, often descend-
ing upon groups of innocent men thought to be the Kellys. Police spies
and informants abounded, and in December, seventy of the Garrison
Artillery were posted in the district to guard the banks.

Those who believed the Kellys were the victims of injustice, however,

CONSTABLE MICHAEL SCANLON, KILLED AT STRINGYBARK CREEK. (POLICE MUSEUM, MELBOURNE)

CONSTABLE THOMAS LONIGAN, KILLED AT STRINGYBARK CREEK. (POLICE MUSEUM, MELBOURNE)

SERGEANT MICHAEL KENNEDY, KILLED AT STRINGYBARK CREEK. (POLICE MUSEUM, MELBOURNE)

CONSTABLE THOMAS MCINTYRE, NED KELLY'S ACCUSER. (POLICE MUSEUM, MELBOURNE)

mostly the selectors and bush workers, reacted somewhat differently. Soon after Stringybark Creek an anonymous bard produced the following composition, a song still in oral tradition during the 1950s when a version was collected in Mansfield by the Rev. Dr Percy Jones:

They had grog and ammunition there to last them many a week,
And next morning two of them rode out all to explore the creek,
Leaving McIntyre behind them at the camp to cook the grub,
And Lonigan to sweep the floor, and boss the washing tub.

It was shortly after breakfast Mac thought he heard a noise,
So gun in hand he sallied out to try and find the cause;
But he never saw the Kellys planted safe behind a log,
So he slithered back to smoke and yarn, and wire into prog [i.e. food].

But bold Kelly and his comrades thought they'd like a nearer look,
For being short of grub, they wished to interview the cook;
And of fire arms and of cartridges they found they had too few,
So they longed to grab the pistols, guns and ammunition too.

Both the bobbies, at the stump alone, they then were pleased to see,
A-watching of the billy boiling for the trooper's tea.
There they smoked and chatted gaily, never thinking of alarms,
Till they heard the fearful cry behind, 'Bail up! Throw up your arms'.

The traps they started wildly, and Mac then firmly stood,
And threw up his arms, while Lonigan made tracks to gain the wood;
Reaching for his revolver, but before he touched the stock,
Ned drew his trigger, and dropped him like a Cock.

Then after searching McIntyre, all through the camp they went
And cleared the guns and cartridges and pistols from the tent;
But brave Kelly muttered sadly as he loaded up his gun,
'Oh, what a _____ pity the _____ tried to run!'[6]

The tone of this song is worlds away from the attitudes expressed in newspapers, such as the *Argus*, which saw the Kellys as part of 'the degraded . . . class of men who hang about bush public houses, or obtain casual employment as station hands'.[7]

'Stringybark Creek' is a good-humoured farce, a piece of black comedy that reflects the antipathy of many selectors and bush itinerants towards officialdom in general and the police in particular. Combined with the local feeling that the police were particularly persecuting the Kellys, and that the fight at Stringybark was a fair one, the actions of the bushrangers were justifiable in terms of self-defence and revenge. This was precisely how Ned described and defended himself in speeches at Euroa, Jerilderie, and Glenrowan, as well as in the Cameron and Jerilderie Letters.

Support and sympathy for the Kellys was far more extensive than the singing of 'Stringybark Creek' and some of the other Kelly songs. The success and survival of the bushrangers for nearly two years was largely a result of their 'bush telegraph' system, the network of family, friends and sympathisers who provided the gang with food, ammunition and information. This system revolved around the nucleus of immediate family and relatives. The cohesion of the Quinns, Kellys and Lloyds, despite their internal disagreements, was the mainstay of the Kelly's bush telegraph.

Each of these families also had many relatives scattered throughout north-eastern Victoria and much further afield, who seem to have aided the bushrangers whenever necessary.[8] There were Quinns near Euroa, in the Strathbogie Ranges, in Mansfield and the surrounding area. Other close relatives of the Kellys lived on Broken River, at Dookie, Lake Rowan and near Mount Look-Out.[9] Superintendent Sadleir considered that there were about one hundred of such sympathisers and telegraphs, not all near-relations: 'But as thick as relations; as loyal to them [the bushrangers] as relations.'[10] There were numerous other important sympathisers not directly related to the Kellys, Quinns or Lloyds

— Ben Gould at Euroa, the McAuliffe family and Edward Burke of Black Range, as well as many others whose names were suppressed, like those of most of the police informers, at the Royal Commission.[11]

And then there were the other members of the gang forged that day at Stringybark Creek, apart from Ned himself. His younger brother, Dan, was only seventeen and had been suspected of horse-stealing at the very tender age of five. Assessments of Dan's character and temperament range from 'quiet and sensitive' to 'a low, cunning sneak'. He had been in trouble with the police, in company with cousins Tom and John Lloyd jun., and spent time in Beechworth gaol. His best mate was Steve Hart, the nineteen-year-old son of a Wangaratta selector, and a superb horseman even by the high standards of the other gang members. Hart was known by the police as a mate of the Kellys and had done time for illegally using horses, but he was not identified as a member of the gang until a few months later when he was recognised during the Euroa bank raid.

Joe Byrne, twenty-one, handsome and popular with women, was also not immediately confirmed as one of the victors at Stringybark Creek. It was a couple of weeks later that his best friend, Aaron Sherritt, accidentally verified Joe's identity to the police. Sherritt would play an increasingly ambiguous role in the Kelly story and would eventually forfeit Joe Byrne's friendship – and his protection.

A fifth man, Tom Lloyd jun., had also been at Stringybark Creek, but he was not seen by McIntyre and so did not become one of the gang. The clan kept his secret and Ned Kelly carried it with him to the grave. Lloyd was never charged with participation in the police murders.[12]

Tom Lloyd was lucky. Like the other four he had served time in gaol for offences involving duffing in one form or another and he knocked around with the Kellys and the other flash tearaways of the region, like 'Wild' Wright and Aaron Sherritt. These young, single men and bush larrikins like them would become solid Kelly sympathisers in the coming months and would feel the wrath of a society which was so determined to protect its laws that it would overturn those laws in north-eastern Victoria.

The history of bushranging legislation amply demonstrates the inability of government to deal with movements of popular protest and resistance within the usual framework of English law. From the early

THE BUSHRANGERS

NED KELLY. (STATE LIBRARY OF VICTORIA ARCHIVES)

JIM KELLY (THE KELLY WHO WAS IN GAOL). (STATE LIBRARY OF VICTORIA ARCHIVES)

DAN KELLY. (POLICE MUSEUM, MELBOURNE)

STEVE HART. (POLICE MUSEUM, MELBOURNE)

JOE BYRNE. (STATE LIBRARY OF VICTORIA ARCHIVES)

convict 'bolters' like Jack Donahue to the 'wild colonial boys' of the 1860s, those in power frequently found it necessary to suspend the normal rights and guarantees provided by law, and to impose restrictions similar to those of a police state.

By 1830 bushrangers like Jack Donahue were so numerous and troublesome in New South Wales that the Legislative Council brought in what came to be unpopularly known as the Bushranging Act. The official title of this legislation was An Act to Suppress Robbery and Housebreaking and the Harbouring of Robbers and Housebreakers.[13] It proclaimed that anyone having reasonable suspicion that a person was carrying firearms to be used for robbery could apprehend that person, without a warrant, and take him before a Justice of the Peace where the person apprehended then had to prove his innocence. If unable to satisfy the justice of either, or both, his identity and innocence, the suspect could be taken to Sydney for closer examination.

Useful though such legislation was in apprehending escaped convicts, many innocent people, both native-born and newly arrived immigrants — most of whom had no formal identification — were continually apprehended without warrants, often dragged to Sydney and held in gaol for long periods without trial until they or someone else could establish their innocence and identity. Not surprisingly, this Act was widely resented and its legality was strongly questioned by both Governor Bourke and Mr Justice Burton. The Governor thought the act 'contrary to the spirit of English law' and Burton stated that it was 'repugnant to the laws of England' in almost all of its provisions.[14] Despite these misgivings, the legislation was re-enacted in various forms almost continuously up to 1853.

By the end of 1864, the failure of the New South Wales police to capture bushrangers protected by strong local support and sympathy, like Ben Hall, Johnny Gilbert, and John Dunn, resulted in public pressure from the respectable classes for 'extreme measures'. On 18 January 1865, the *Sydney Morning Herald* published Chief Justice Stephen's considered suggestions for effective bushranging legislation. This lengthy piece of legalese basically advocated the outlawry of selected bushrangers, rendering them liable to be shot on sight by police or civilians. Sympathisers were to be apprehended only on the accusation of a policeman or citizen.

On 8 April 1865, these suggestions were given official sanction under the title of the Felons Apprehension Act and became effective from 10 May. Gilbert and Dunn (Hall was killed two days before the proclamation of outlawry) were liable to be shot by anyone. Persons suspected of harbouring could be arrested and presumed guilty on the most flimsy evidence, and liable to forfeit all their goods and land as well as serving up to fifteen years in gaol with hard labour. A Justice of the Peace or police officer could enter, without a warrant, any dwelling suspected of harbouring bushrangers. Finally the police, if they were pursuing bushrangers, were empowered to commandeer horses, equipment, or supplies.[15] As a *Sydney Morning Herald* editorial put it: 'The Felons Apprehension Act . . . has shown that the general public is resolved to re-establish order and security, even at the risk of temporarily impairing the liberty of the subject.'[16]

The Victorian government of 1878, when faced with the same predicament, was no more able to resolve it within the normal legal framework than the New South Wales government. The Victorian Felons Apprehension Act became law and two months later its provisions were used to subvert the liberty of selected individuals. Beginning on 2 January 1879, the police arrested thirty suspected Kelly sympathisers and lodged them in Beechworth gaol. Twenty-three were charged and over the next four months many of these unfortunates were continually remanded in custody while the court awaited the presentation of police evidence against them. By 22 April eleven men were still inside the gaol without having had any police case laid against them. Finally, an embarrassed presiding magistrate could no longer ignore the blatant illegality of the situation and released the prisoners.

Among the suspected sympathisers arrested by the desperate police force, some like Tom Lloyd and Isaiah 'Wild' Wright were definitely members of the Kellys' bush telegraph. But there were quite a few who just as definitely were not, such as Jackie McMonigal who merely worked with Ned in the sawmills earlier in the 1870s. The period during which these men were locked up coincided with harvest-time, and many families consequently experienced great difficulty and hardship getting their crops in. Not surprisingly, this whole episode further alienated both sympathisers and non-sympathisers from the police and their whole campaign. Coupled with this policy of intimidation the police could, and did, ensure that suspected sympathisers were prevented from selecting land needed to extend their farms.

The incarceration of twenty-odd men hardly affected the bush telegraph. Even though two important sympathisers, Tom Lloyd and 'Wild' Wright, were out of action, the police had no luck in their continued pursuit of the bushrangers. Sympathisers still provided horses, food, shelter, ammunition, and intelligence of police movements to the gang.[17] They also carried out the undoubtedly pleasurable task of providing the police with false information concerning the activities of the outlaws.[18] Of the one hundred and twenty-seven reported sightings of the Kellys between November 1878 and April 1879, not one of those followed up by the police yielded even a glimpse of the gang.[19] This was the result of false information, police bungling, and the prearranged system of warning signals that the telegraphs used to inform the bushrangers of police presence.[20] Apart from Glenrowan, which was supposed to have been a trap for the police, the only other contact that members of the force had with the bushrangers was at Stringybark Creek, an engagement which the Kellys definitely won.

At the other end of Victorian society, the law-abiding classes expressed their disgust not only at the murders but also at the disturbing extent of sympathy for the Kellys. The existence of a group of hereditary criminals, setting the law at defiance and aided by a vast network of sympathisers, was seen as a positive danger to the character and social stability of Victoria. So great were the apparent dangers of such a situation that the suspension of the legal rights of individuals was not merely necessary but absolutely justifiable. This withdrawal of the forms of liberty from 'degraded' men was seen to be the means of maintaining the substance of liberty for the 'respectable portion of society'.[21] No consideration was given to the possibility that such strong and extensive manifestations of sympathy for a gang of bushrangers might indicate the existence of more fundamental discontents than those which produced mere criminality.

During the periods of the Kellys' main activities, October 1878 to March 1879, and June to November 1880, the Melbourne press would scarcely publish an issue that did not contain some reference to the outlaws and their sympathisers. The continued failure of the police to catch the bushrangers was increasingly criticised in editorials and letters.

Frequent references were made to the seemingly vast sympathy that the Kellys enjoyed in the north-eastern district, even in 'respectable' quarters. Concerned correspondents offered various suggestions for the capture of the Kellys,[22] and one gentleman suggested that the government 'suspend the Habeas Corpus Act for a time in that locality, arrest every man, woman and youth suspected of favouring the murderers, and keep them in durance until the murderers are either captured or shot'.[23]

The following month, the editor of the *Argus* doubted that the suspension of Habeas Corpus in the north-east was necessary as the police could do whatever was needed under the provisions of the *Felons Apprehension Act 1878*.[24] The sympathisers gaoled and remanded at Beechworth were victims of the Outlawry Act, and the illegality of their incarceration was the direct result of the way in which those who made and administered the law perceived the outbreak.

In the course of justifying the Beechworth court's denial of justice to the imprisoned sympathisers, the *Argus* urged the Victorian Parliament to pass an Act of Indemnity:

> No doubt this would be a high-handed proceeding, but it would be one of those arbitrary courses which are sometimes essential to the existence of real liberty. When the freedom and property of quiet and respectable people are endangered by the immunity enjoyed by scoundrels, under the forms of law, common sense and social interests require that the convenience of the Isaiah Wrights should be subordinated to the well-being of the decent portion of the community.[25]

A few months earlier, the same paper had commented that: 'When we find half a district sympathising with murderers and the other half reduced to silence and inaction through fear it is no time to stand upon ceremony.'[26]

As with earlier bushrangers, the view was expressed that the Kellys were a blot upon the reputation of a British colony: 'A community of Englishmen will not long suffer it to be known that a handful of armed men, however desperate and daring, can murder at will.'[27] One anxious correspondent thought that: 'We must clear the colony of the scourge, or our reputation will suffer in the eyes of the world.'[28] Though not as strongly or consistently expressed as in New South Wales during the

1860s, this feeling about the desirable British character of the colony remained a constant element in the views of the respectable portion of society.

In 1879, a gang of four bushrangers began impersonating the Kellys in New South Wales. When they were finally captured, the *Argus* rejoiced that this had 'relieved us from the fear of an outbreak'. This expression of relief was preceded by a discussion of Frank Gardiner and Johnny Gilbert as instigators of the bushranging epidemic of the 1860s.[29] A comforting analogy was drawn between the successful growth of Gilbert and Gardiner imitations in the 1860s and the early apprehension of Kelly-imitators: ' . . . now, though the original desperadoes are still at large, we may reasonably hope that a war against society will not be waged in any other part of the land.'[30]

These fears proved to be unfounded. No subsequent bushranging outbreaks occurred, and the authorities were free to concentrate their efforts upon rooting out the 'tribe of hardened criminals who had taken possession of the land and for years defied the law'.[31] And although the *Argus* doubted that 'the Dick Turpin and Jack Sheppard sentiment had any serious prevalence in the land', two days later the same writer was complaining that Kelly sympathisers were everywhere, and aiding the bushrangers so effectively that they should all be arrested.[32]

Of course, this extensive network of sympathisers needed financing in order to continue for more than a few months. Aiding the Kelly gang was expensive, and the main sympathisers were not, almost by definition, people of substance. The proceeds of the Euroa and Jerilderie robberies soon turned up in general circulation throughout the Kelly country. Joe Byrne's family experienced a visible increase in material wealth after the gang's subsequent bank robberies, though most of the money seems to have gone towards the cost of keeping the bushrangers armed and fed.

Robbing banks was the most immediate means of securing money. To the Kellys and their sympathisers this had the additional advantage of striking at the enemy's resources. The bushrangers would then be able to maintain both themselves and their 'Robin Hood' image, ensuring continued local support and sympathy. Their first bank hold-up was in a small sleepy town near the southern extremity of the Kelly country, barely six weeks after Stringybark Creek.

CHAPTER
5

'I WILL OPPOSE YOUR LAWS'

A little more than a month after the Kelly brothers and their two companions were outlawed, they began to act in a manner befitting bandits. Four miles outside the small town of Euroa was a substantial property, Younghusband's Faithfull Creek station — just 'Younghusband's' to the locals. It was here that the bushrangers introduced themselves to the employees on the morning of 9 December 1878. The subsequent proceedings were quite civilised, though firmly carried through by the Kellys. All the station-hands were taken into custody while the bushrangers made themselves at home for the remainder of that day and the following night.

The women present were treated with great respect and civility by the gang in the best highwayman style, and although the men were locked in the storeroom for the night, their captivity was eased with a fine meal prepared by Mrs Fitzgerald, the station cook (she was a Kelly sympathiser), and by what must have been a fascinating few hours of conversation with Ned Kelly himself. As would become usual on these occasions, Ned spoke grimly of the police persecution of his family, particularly his mother, and also discussed his duffing prowess and the fight at Stringybark Creek. The question that must have been in the minds of all present had to wait until the following day for an answer.

One late-comer was a hawker, complete with his wares of clothes and arms. This proved to be extremely convenient for the bushrangers who were able to change out of their ragged bush-clothes and into some decent town-clothes for the job they had to do in Euroa.

The next day, after cutting down the telegraph wires into and out of town, and adding even more captives to the now-crowded storeroom, including a linesman and four railway workers sent to repair the telegraph line, Ned, Dan and Steve Hart dressed themselves in their respectable new clothes. Leaving Joe Byrne at the station to guard the prisoners, they set off for the town in two carts.

It was licence day at Euroa, and the sole constable was otherwise occupied. After spying out the town, the bushrangers parked their carts at the back and front of the bank. The manager, Mr Scott, his wife and family, together with the accountant and two clerks, were politely bailed up and the bank's strongroom relieved of over £2000 in cash and gold — a lot of money at that time. Ned also took a number of mortgages from the bank, leaving most of the securities and the like behind.

As the bank was officially closed, the robbery proceeded without a hitch. Everyone in the bank was 'invited' to attend a party at Younghusband's station, to which they would be most willingly escorted by the bushrangers. The crowd of people who left town with the bushrangers included the manager's wife and seven children, household servants, and bank employees. They attracted no interest at all.[1] It was eleven o'clock at night before the townspeople found out that their bank had been robbed. The only ones who did know were the Kellys and the thirty-seven prisoners they held at Younghusband's.

Ned had supper prepared for all his 'guests', after which Dan and Steve gave an exhibition of horsemanship and Ned made another speech about the persecution of himself and his family. After warning that no one leave the station for at least three hours, the bushrangers made off as suddenly as they had arrived. Over the next few weeks a lot of the Kellys' poor friends in north-eastern Victoria were able to pay some of their debts, and to run up more in the public houses. As Mrs Scott later recalled: 'They took a great deal of silver from Euroa and a fairly large account was paid next day by one of their friends, in sixpences and shillings.'[2]

The police were helpless, unable to get even a smell of the gang except for false leads that started them on wild-goose chases, including one across the Murray into New South Wales. The press, adopting a tone that would become the norm during the outbreak, raged against the ineptitude of the police[3] and the daring of the Kellys: '... the whole country is in the hands of an extensive criminal community, who do not hesitate to impudently manifest their power', thundered an *Age* editorial.[4] Less than two months later the Kellys were to 'impudently manifest their power' yet again. But before that, a document cataloguing the popular grievances of the north-eastern district appeared in the form of a letter from Ned Kelly himself, given to Mrs Fitzgerald just before the gang galloped away from Younghusband's station.

The 'Cameron Letter' gained its unexciting title from the name of the MLA to whom it was addressed, Mr Donald Cameron, who had opposed the Felons Apprehension Act in the Victorian Parliament. Posted at Glenrowan, four days after the Euroa raid, the letter sets out the Kellys' complaints probably in much the same manner as Ned addressed his captive audience at Younghusband's station. The letter is printed here with the original spelling and punctuation.

THE CAMERON LETTER

Dear Sir,

Take no offence if I take the opportunity of writing a few lines to you wherein I wish to state a few remarks concerning the case of Trooper Fitzpatrick against Mrs. Kelly W. Skillion and W. Williamson and to state the facts of the case to you.

It seems impossible for me to get any justice without I make a statement to some one that will take notice of it as it is no use in me complaining about anything that the Police may choose to say or swear against me and the public in their ignorance and blindness will undoubtedly back them up to their utmost.

No doubt I am now placed in very peculiar circumstances and you might blame me for it but if you knew how I have been wronged and persecuted you would say I cannot be blamed.

In April last an information was (which must have come under your notice) sworn against me for shooting trooper Fitzpatrick which was false and my mother with an infant baby and brother-in-law and another neighbour was taken for aiding and abetting and attempting to murder him a charge of they are as purely innocent as the child unborn.

During my stay on the King River I run in a wild bull which I gave to Lydicher who afterwards sold him to Carr and he killed him for beef.

Sometime afterwards I was told I was blamed for stealing this bull from Whitty I asked Whitty on Moyhu racecourse why he blamed me for stealing his bull he said he had his bull and **he** never blamed me for stealing him.

He said it was Farrel who told him that I stole the bull. Sometime afterwards I heard again I was blamed for stealing a mob of calves from Whitty and Farrell which I never had anything to do with and along with this and other talk I began to think they wanted something to talk about.

Whitty and Burns not being satisfied with all the picked land on King River and Boggy Creek and the run of their stock on the certificate ground free and no one interferring with them. Paid heavy rent for all the open ground so as a poor man could not keep any stock and impounded every beast they could catch even off government roads if a poor man happened to leave his horse or bit of poddy calf outside his paddock it would be impounded.

I have known over 60 head of horses to be in one day impounded by Whitty and Burns all belonging to poor men of the district they would have to leave their harvest or ploughing and go to Oxley and then perhaps not have enough money to release them and have to give a bill of sale or borrow the money which is no easy matter and along with all this sort of work Farrell the Policeman stole a horse from George King and had him in Whitty and Jeffrey's paddock until he left the force and this was the cause of me and my stepfather George King stealing Whitty's horses and selling them to Baumgarten and those other men the pick of them was sold to Howlong and the rest was sold to Baumgarten who was a perfect stranger to me and I believe an honest man.

No man had anything to do with the horses but me and George King[.] William Cooke who was convicted for Whitty's horses had nothing to do with them nor was he ever in my company at Peterson the German's at Howlong.

The brands was altered by me and George King and the horses were sold as straight.

Anyman requiring horses would have bought them the same as those men and would have potted the same and I consider Whitty ought to do something towards the release of those innocent men otherwise there will be a collision between me and him as I can to his satisfaction prove I took J Welshe's black mare and the rest of the horses which I will prove to him in next issue and after those horses had been found and the row being over them I wrote a letter to Mr. Swannell of Lake Rowan to advertise my horses for sale as I was intend[ing] to sell out.

I sold them afterwards at Benalla and the rest in New South Wales and left Victoria as I wished to see certain parts of the country and very shortly afterward there was a warrant for me and as I since hear the Police Sergeant Steel, Straughan and Fitzpatrick and others searched the Seven Mile and every other place in the district for me and a man named Newman who had escaped from the Wangaratta Police for months before the 15th of April. Therefore it was impossible for me to be in Victoria as every schoolboy knows me and on the 15th of April Fitzpatrick came to the Seven Mile and had some conversation with Williamson who was splitting [timber] on the hill seeing my brother and another man he rode down and had some conversation with this man whom he swore was William Skillion this man was not called in Beechworth as he could have proved Fitzpatrick's falsehood as Skillion and another man was away after horses at this time which can be proved by eight or nine witnesses the man who the trooper swore was Skillion can prove Williamson's innocence besides other important evidence which can be brought on the prisoners behalf.

The trooper after speaking to this man rode to the house and Dan came out he asked Dan to go to Greta with him Dan asked what for and he said he had a warrant for him for stealing Whitty's horses.

They both went inside Dan was having something to eat the trooper was impatient and Mrs. Kelly asked him what he wanted Dan for and he said he had a warrant for him.

Dan said produce your warrant and he said he had none it was only a telegram from Chiltern.

Mrs Kelly said he need not go unless he liked without a warrant. She told him the trooper had no business on her premises without some authority besides his own word.

He pulled out his revolver and said he would blow her brains out if she interfered in the arrest Mrs Kelly said if Ned was here he would ram the revolver down his throat.

To frighten the trooper Dan said Ned is coming now. The trooper looked around to see if it was true Dan dropped his knife and fork which shewed he had no murderous intention clapped Heenan's hug on him took his revolver and threw him and part of the door outside and kept him there until Skillion and Ryan came with horses which Dan sold that night the trooper left and invented some scheme to say he got shot which any man can see it is impossible for him to have been shot. He told Dan to clear out that Sergeant Steel or Detective Brown would be there before morning as Straughan was over the Murray trying to get up a case against Dan and the Lloyds as the Germans over the Murray would swear to any one and they will lag you guilty or not.

Next day Skillion, Williamson and Mrs. Kelly with an infant were taken and thrown into prison and were six months awaiting trial and no bail allowed and was convicted on the evidence of the meanest man that ever the sun shone on I have been told by Police that he is hardly ever sober also between him and his father they sold his sister to a Chinaman but he seems a strapping and rather genteel looking young man more fit to be a starcher to a laundry than a trooper, but to a keen observer he has the wrong appearance to have anything like a clear conscience or a manly heart the deceit is too plain to be seen in the white cabbage hearted looking face.

I heard nothing of this transaction until very close on the trial I being then over 400 miles from Greta.

I heard I was outlawed and £100 reward for me in Victoria and also hundreds of charges of horsestealing was against me besides shooting a trooper.

I came into Victoria and enquired after my brother and found him working with another man on Bullock Creek.

Heard how the Police used to be blowing [i.e. boasting] that they would shoot me first and then cry surrender.

How they used to come to the house when there was no one there but women and Superintendent Smith used to say see all the men I have out today I will have as many more tomorrow and blow him into pieces as small as paper that is in our guns and they used to repeatedly rush into the house revolver in hand upset milk dishes empty the flour out on the ground break tins of eggs and even throw the meat out of the cask on to the floor and dirty and destroy all the provisions which can be proved and shove the girls in front of them into the rooms like dogs and abuse and insult them. Detective Ward and Constable Hayes took out their revolvers and threatened to shoot the girls and children whilst Mrs Skillion was absent, the oldest being with her.

The greatest murders [*sic*] and ruffians would not be guilty of such an action.

This sort of cruelty and disgraceful conduct to my brothers and sisters who had no protection coupled with the conviction of my mother and those innocent men certainly made my blood boil and I don't think there is any man born could have the patience to suffer what I did.

They were not satisfied with frightening and insulting my sisters night and day and destroying their provisions and lagging my mother with an infant baby and those innocent men but should follow me and my brother who was innocent of having anything to do with any stolen horses into the wilds where he had been quietly digging and doing well neither molesting or interfering with any one.

And I was not there long and on the 25th of October I came on the tracks of Police horses between tabletop and the boys I crossed them and went to Emu Swamp and returning home I came on more Police tracks making for our camp.

I told my mates and me and my brother went out next morning and found Police camped at the shingle hut with long firearms and we came to the conclusion our doom was sealed unless we could take their firearms, as we had nothing but a gun and a rifle, if they came on us at our work or camp we had no chance only to die like dogs as we thought the country was woven with Police and we might have a chance of fighting them if we had firearms as it generally takes 40 to one.

AN EARLY KELLY REWARD POSTER. (POLICE MUSEUM, MELBOURNE)

We approached the spring as close as we could get to the camp. The intervening space being clear we saw two men at the top they got up and one took a double barrel fowling piece and one drive the horses down and hobled them against the tent and we thought there was more men in the tent those being on sentry. We could have shot those two men without speaking but not wishing to take life we waited McIntyre laid the gun against the stump Lonigan sat on the log I advanced my brother Dan keeping McIntyre covered I called on them to throw up their hands McIntyre obeyed and never attempted to reach for his gun or revolver.

Lonigan ran to a battery of logs and put his head up to take aim at me when I shot him or he would have shot me as I knew well I asked who was in the tent McIntyre replied no one.

I approached the camp and took possession of their revolvers and fowling piece which I loaded with bullets instead of shot I told McIntyre I did not want to shoot him or any man that would surrender I explained Fitzpatrick's falsehood which no policeman can be ignorant of.

He said he knew Fitzpatrick had wronged us but he could not help it. He said he intended to leave the force on account of his bad health his life was insured the other two men who had no firearms came up

V. R.

£8000 REWARD

ROBBERY and MURDER.

WHEREAS EDWARD KELLY, DANIEL KELLY, STEPHEN HART, and JOSEPH BYRNE have been declared OUTLAWS in the Colony of Victoria, and whereas warrants have been issued charging the above-named men with the WILFUL MURDER of MICHAEL SCANLON, Police Constable of the Colony of VICTORIA, and whereas the above-named offenders are STILL at LARGE and have recently committed divers felonies in the Colony of NEW SOUTH WALES: Now, therefore, I, SIR HERCULES GEORGE ROBERT ROBINSON, the GOVERNOR, &c. by this, my proclamation issued with the advice of the Executive Council, hereby notify that a REWARD of £4,000 will be paid, three-fourths by the Government of NEW SOUTH WALES, and one-fourth by certain Banks trading in the Colony, for the apprehension of the above-named Four Offenders, or a reward of £1000 for the apprehension of any one of them, and that in ADDITION to the above reward a similar REWARD of £4000 has been offered by the Government of VICTORIA, and I further notify that the said REWARD will be equitably apportioned between any persons giving information which shall lead to the apprehension of the offenders and any members of the police force or other persons who may actually effect such apprehension or assist thereat.

(Signed) HENRY PARKES,
Colonial Secretary, New South Wales.

(Signed) BRYAN O'LOGHLEN,
Attorney-General, Victoria.

Dated 15th February, 1879.

THE LAST KELLY REWARD POSTER. (STATE LIBRARY OF VICTORIA ARCHIVES)

when they heard the shot fired, and went back to our camp for fear the Police might call there in our absence and surprise us on our arrival.

My brother went back to the spring and I stopped at the top with McIntyre, Kennedy and Scanlan came up, McIntyre said he would get them to surrender if I spared their lives as well as his, I said I did not know either him Scanlan or Kennedy and had nothing against them and would not shoot any of them if they gave up their firearms and promise to leave the force as it was the meanest billet in the world they are worse than cold blooded murderers or hangmen.

He said he was sure they would never follow me any more. I gave him my word I would give them a chance McIntyre went up to Kennedy Scanlan being behind with a rifle and a revolver I called on them to throw up their hands Scanlan slewed his horse around to gallop away but turned again, and as quick as thought fired at me with the rifle and was in the act of firing again when I shot him.

Kennedy alighted on the off side of his horse and got behind a tree and opened hot fire McIntyre got on Kennedy's horse and galloped away.

I could have shot him if I choose as he was right against me but rather than break my word I let him go.

My brother advanced from the spring Kennedy fired at him and ran as he found neither of us was dead.

I followed him he got behind another tree and fired at me again. I shot him in the arm-pit as he was behind the tree he dropped his revolver and ran again and slewed round and I fired with the gun again and shot him through the right chest as I did not know he had dropped his revolver and was turning to surrender he could not live or I would have let him go.

Had they been my own brothers I could not help shooting them, or else lie down and let them shoot me which they would have done had their bullets been directed as they intended them.

But as for handcuffing Kennedy to a tree or cutting his ear off, or brutally treating any one them, is a cruel falsehood.

If Kennedy's ear was cut off it has been done since. I put his cloak over him and left him as honourable as I could and if they were my own brothers I could not be more sorry for them with the exception of Lonigan I did not begrudge him what bit of lead he got as he was the flashest and meanest man that I had any account against him Fitzpatrick Sergeant Whelan Constable O'Day and King the bootmaker once tried to handcuff me at Benalla and when they could not Fitzpatrick tried to choke me. Lonigan caught me by the privates and would have killed me but was not able Mr McInnis came up and I allowed him to put the handcuffs on when the Police were bested.

This cannot be called wilful murder for I was compelled to shoot them in my own defence or lie down like a cur and die.

Certainly their wives and children are to be pitied but those men came into the bush with the intention of shooting me down like a dog and yet they know and acknowledge I have been wronged.

And is my mother and her infant baby and my poor little brothers and sisters not to be pitied moreso who has got no alternative only to put up with brutal and unmanly conduct of the Police who have never had any relation or a mother or must have forgot them I was never convicted of horsestealing I was once arrested by Constable Hall and 14 more men in Greta and there was a subscription raised for Hall by persons who had too much money about Greta in honour of Hall arresting Wild Wright and Gunn.

Wright and Gunn were potted [i.e. jailed] and Hal could not pot me for horsestealing but with the subscription money he gave £20 to James Murdock who has recently been hung in Wagga Wagga and on Murdock's evidence I was found guilty of receiving knowing to be stolen which I Wright W. Ambrose J. Ambrose and W. Hatcher and W. Williamson and others can prove I was innocent of Knowing the mare to be stolen and I was once accused of taking a hawker of the name of McCormacks horse [i.e. a horse belonging to a hawker named McCormack] to pull another hawker named Ben Gould out of a bog.

Mr Gould got up in the morning to feed his horses seen McCormack's horse and knew he had strayed sent his man in with him about two miles to where McCormack was camped in Greta.

Mr & Mrs McCormack came out and seen the waggons bogged and accused him of using the horse.

I told Gould that was for his good nature Mrs McCormack turned on me and accused me for catching the horse for Gould as Gould knew he was wicked and could not catch him himself. Me and my uncle was cutting and branding calves and Ben Gould wrapped up a pair of testicles wrote a note and gave it to me to give to Mrs McCormack McCormack said he would fight me I was then 14 years of age, I was getting off my horse and Mrs McCormack hit the horse he jumped forwards and my fist came in collision with McCormack's nose who swore he was standing 10 yards away from another man and the one hit knocked two men down, however ridiculous the evidence may seem I received 3 months or 10£ fine for hitting him and 3 months for delivering the parcel and bound to the peace for 12 months.

At the time I was taken by Hall and his 14 assistants, therefore I dare not strike any of them as Hall was a great cur, and as for Dan he never was tried for assaulting a woman Mr Butler PM sentenced him to 3 months without the option of a fine and one month or two pounds fine for wilfully destroying property a sentence which there is no law to uphold and yet they had to do their sentences and their prosecutor Mr D Goodman since got 4 years for perjury concerning the same property.

The Minister of justice should enquire into this respecting their sentence and he will find a wrong jurisdiction given by Butler P.M. on the 19th of October 1877 1877 at Benalla.

And these are the only charges was ever proved against either of us therefore we are falsely represented.

The report of bullets having being fired into the bodies of the troopers after their death is false and the coroner should be consulted I have no intention of asking mercy for myself of any mortal man, or apologising, but I wish to give timely warning that if my people do not get justice and those innocents released from prison and the Police wear their uniforms I shall be forced to seek revenge of everything of the human race for the future.

I will not take innocent life if justice is given but as it is the Police are afraid or ashamed to wear their uniform therefore every mans life is in danger as I was outlawed without any cause and cannot be no worse and have but once to die and if the public do not see justice done I will seek revenge for the name and character which has been given to me and my relations while God gives me strength to pull a trigger.

The witnesses which can prove Fitzpatrick's falsehood can be found by advertising and if this is not done immediately horrible disasters will follow. Fitzpatrick shall be the cause of greater slaughter to the rising generation than St. Patrick was to the snakes and frogs in Ireland.

For had I robbed, plundered, ravished and murdered everything I met my character could not be painted blacker than it is at present but thank God my conscience is as clear as the snow in Peru and as I hear a picked jury amongst which was a discharged Sergeant of Police was impanelled on the trial and David Lindsay who gave evidence for the Crown is a shantykeeper having no license and is liable to a heavy fine and keeps a book of information for the Police and his character needs no comment for he is capable of rendering Fitzpatrick any assistance he required for a conviction as he could be broke any time Fitzpatrick chose to inform on him.

I am really astonished to see members of the Legislative Assembly led astray by such articles as the Police for while an outlaw reigns their pocket swells, Tis double pay and country girls.

By concluding as I have no more paper unless I rob for it, if I get justice I will cry a go.

For I need no lead or powder to revenge my cause, and if words be louder I will oppose your laws.

With no offence (remember your railroads) and a sweet good bye from

> Edward Kelly
> a forced outlaw

The Cameron Letter is a draft version of the more famous and more interesting Jerilderie Letter. Many sections prefigure, almost word for word, passages in the Jerilderie Letter. Kelly's grievances are the same as those complained of in the later document; police harassment and persecution, the practice of impounding, and the inequity of the land system in general. A good deal of the Cameron Letter is devoted to the bushrangers' version of the Stringybark Creek fight, and Ned ends by appealing for 'a go'.

But he was not to get one, and the drama moved inexorably towards the next act. Before it could begin, however, a new song registered popular reaction to the events at Euroa. Not surprisingly, its tone was a little different to that of the press and the government. 'Sticking Up of the Euroa Bank' delights in the spectacle of a trembling bank manager and the outlaws' 'glorious haul':

STICKING UP OF THE EUROA BANK

So Kelly marched into the bank,
A cheque all in his hand,
For to have it changed for money
Of Scott he did demand.

And when that he refused him,
He, looking at him straight,
Said, 'See here my name's Ned Kelly
And this here man's my mate.'

With pistols pointed at his nut,
Poor Scott did stand amazed,
His stick he would have liked to cut,
But was with funk half crazed.

The poor cashier with real fear,
Stood trembling at the knees,
But at last both seen 'twas no use
And handed out the keys.

The safe was quickly gutted then
The drawers turned out as well,
The Kellys being quite polite,
Like any noble swell.

With flimsies, gold and silver coin,
The threepennies and all,
Amounting to two thousand pounds
They made a glorious haul![5]

CHAPTER
6

'I AM A WIDOW'S SON OUTLAWED'

I t was almost midnight on Saturday, 8 February 1879. The two policemen who constituted the Jerilderie (NSW) police force heard someone beating on the station door and shouting about a fight at one of the town's six hotels. They opened the door and discovered that the Kelly gang had crossed the border to visit them. Senior Constable Devine and Constable Richards were manacled with their own handcuffs and locked in their own cells. The policemen and Devine's wife, who also lived at the station, were informed that no one would be harmed as long as they did as they were told. Ned made a special point of informing them that the bushrangers would not molest Mrs Devine, or any other woman.[1]

The next morning, making full use of the facilities of the New South Wales police, the bushrangers dressed themselves in troopers' uniforms. Dan escorted Mrs Devine to the courthouse to prepare it for mass, one of many actions at Jerilderie to become immortalised by the popular muse in 'The Ballad of the Kelly Gang'.

In the afternoon Ned and Joe were audacious enough to have Constable Richards accompany them on a stroll through the town and have him explain them to passing townspeople as a special anti-Kelly police squad. They then casually returned to the lock-up for the evening.

At noon the next day the gang had Constable Richards introduce

67

them to the incredulous publican of the Royal Mail Hotel. Everyone in the vicinity was herded into the bar and the drinks were on the Kellys. But the bushrangers' interest in the Royal Hotel was more than social. The local branch of the Bank of New South Wales was part of the same building and it was not long before Ned and Joe excused themselves from the bar, went into the bank, and invited the two bank clerks, the manager, and an astonished customer to join the party at the Royal Hotel — though not before they had 'withdrawn' over £2000, after relieving the manager of the safe keys while the unfortunate man was helpless in his bath.

Ned also burned the mortgages and some ledgers to the lusty cheers of the crowd in the hotel who were enthused by sympathy, fear, alcohol, or a combination of all three. According to one eye-witness, the bush-ranger commented that the banks were crushing the life's-blood out of the poor struggling man and this was a good reason for destroying all the mortgages.[2]

Ned Kelly then went to find the Jerilderie printer, saying that he wanted to have a letter published, but the printer could not be found. He was hiding in a drain outside the town, fearful that the Kellys had come to murder him. Instead, the manuscript was entrusted to Living, one of the bank clerks. The document would soon become known as the Jerilderie Letter.

Then Kelly returned to the hotel where Dan and Steve were keep-ing their eyes on more than thirty prisoners. Joe Byrne had already taken the money and supplies and left, after destroying the telegraph link. Steve Hart helped himself to a Presbyterian minister's watch, say-ing 'a poor parson is nothing to me'.[3] Ned, ever the PR man, made him return it, whereupon Steve took the publican's watch which Ned likewise demanded that he return. One account says that Hart also took the bank manager's watch and was surprised to find that such an eminent person possessed only a silver timepiece.[4] Ned Kelly gave his standard speech for such occasions, stressing the injustice he and his peers had suffered and the general villainy of the police force. The three bushrangers mounted up and Steve Hart completed the show with a display of horsemanship. Before riding off in the direction of Urana, they told the Jerilderie townspeople that they intended to rob the mail coach there. Of course, they headed straight back across the Murray leaving the people of New South Wales with something to gossip about for years to come. Soon after the bushrangers' departure the unusually large number of 'strangers' seen in Jerilderie before and during the robbery also faded away.[5]

The New South Wales government, under pressure from the Bank of New South Wales, reversed their earlier refusal to offer a reward for the Kellys and matched the £4000 offered by the Victorian government. The gang was now worth a total of £8000, dead or alive, an amount generally considered to be the largest ever offered for bandits. But in spite of this, and frantic police activity on both sides of the border, the Kellys could not be found anywhere, though the Kelly country received another sudden economic stimulus in the form of crisp New South Wales banknotes.

In the meantime, a different kind of note, the Jerilderie Letter, was being copied and bowdlerised by a Victorian government clerk. The complete original text of the letter was not published until relatively recently and the original, like Ned Kelly's armour, long mysteriously disappeared, has surfaced again. Here is the version that has come down to us as the authentic item, once again with the original spelling and punctuation:

THE JERILDERIE LETTER

(Page 1)

Dear Sir,

I wish to acquaint you with some of the occurrences of the present past and future.

In or about the spring, of 1870 the ground was very soft a hawker named Mr Gould got his waggon bogged between Greta and my mother's house on the eleven mile creek, the ground was that rotten it would bog a duck in places so Mr Gould had abandon his waggon for fear of loosing his horses in the spewy ground he was stopping at my mothers awaiting finer or dryer weather Mr McCormack and his wife hawkers also were camped in Greta the mosquitoes were very bad which they generally are in a wet spring and to help them

(Page 2)

Mr Johns had a horse called ruita cruta although a gelding was as clever as old Wombat or any other stallion at running horses away and taking them on his beat which was from Greta swamp to the seven mile creek consequently he enticed McCormacks horse away from Greta.

Mr Gould was up early feeding his horses heard a bell and seen McCormack horses for he knew the horse well he sent his boy to take him back to Greta.

When McCormack's got the horse they came straight out to Goold and accused him of working the horse; this was false and Goold was amazed at the idea I could not help laughing to hear Mrs McCormack

(Page 3)

accusing him of using the horse after him being so kind as to send his boy to take him from the ruta cruta and take him back to them.

I pleaded Goulds innocence and Mrs McCormack turned on me and accused me of bringing the horse from Greta to Goold's wagon to pull him out of the bog I did not say much to the woman as my mother was present but the same day me and my uncle was cutting calves Gould wrapped up a note and a pair of the calves testicles and gave them to me to give them to Mrs McCormack. I did not see her and gave the parcel to a boy to give to her when she would come instead of giving it

(Page 4)

to her he gave it to her husband consequently McCormack said he would summons me I told him neither me or Gould used their horse.

he said I was a liar & he could welt me or any of my breed I was about 14 years of age but accepted the challenge and dismounting when Mrs McCormack struck my horse in the flank with a bullocks skin it jumped forward and my fist came in collision with McCormack's nose and caused him to loose his equilibrium and fall postrate I tied up my horse to finish the battle but McCormack got up and ran to the Police camp.

Constable Hall asked me what the row was about. I told him they

(Page 5)

accused me and Gould of using their horse and I hit him and would do the same to him if he challenged me. McCormack pulled me and swore their lies against me.

I was sentenced to three months for hitting him and three months for the parcel and bound to keep the peace for 12 months.

Mrs McCormack gave good substantial evidence as she is well acquainted with that place called Tasmania better known as the Dervon or Vandiemans land and McCormack being a Police man over the convicts and women being scarce released from that land of bondage and tyranny, and they came to

(Page 6)

Victoria and are at present residents of Greta and on the 29th of March I was released from prison and came home Wild Wright came to the eleven mile to see Mr Gunn stopped all night and lost his mare both him and me looked all day for her and could not get her Wright who was a stranger to me was in a hurry to get back to Mansfield and I gave him another mare and he told me if I found his mare to keep her until he brought mine back.

I was going to Wangaratta and seen the mare and I caught her and took her with me all the Police and Detective Berrill seen her as Martans girls used to ride her about

(Page 7)

the town during several days that I stopped at Petre Martains Star Hotel in Wangaratta, she was a chestnut mare white face docked tail very remarkable branded (M) as plain as the hands on a town clock, the property of a Telegraph Master in Mansfield, he lost her on the 6th gazetted her on the 12th of March and I was a prisoner in Beechworth Gaol until the 29 of March therefore I could not have stole the mare.

I was riding the mare through Greta Constable Hall came to me and said he wanted me to sign some papers that I did not sign at Beechworth concerning my bail bonds I thought it was the truth he said the papers was at the Barracks and I had no idea he wanted to arrest me or I

(Page 8)

would have quietly rode away instead of going to the Barracks.

I was getting off when Hall caught hold of me and thought to throw me but made a mistake and came on the broad of his back himself in the dust the mare galloped away and instead of me putting my foot on Halls neck and taking his revolver and putting him in the lock up. I tried to catch the mare. Hall got up and snapped three or four caps at me and would have shot me but the colts patent refused.

This is well known in Greta Hall never told me he wanted to arrest me until after he tried to shoot me when I heard the caps snapping I stood until Hall came close he had me covered and was shaking with fear and I knew he would pull the

(Page 9)

trigger before he would be game to put his hand on me so I duped and jumped at him caught the revolver with one hand and Hall by the collar with the other.

I dare not strike him or my sureties would loose the bond money I used to trip him and let him take a mouth ful of dust now and again as he was as helpless as a big guano after leaving a dead bullock or a horse. I kept throwing him in the dust until I got him across the street the very spot where Mrs O'Brien's Hotel stands now the cellar was just dug then there was some brush fencing where the post and rail was taking down and on this I threw big cowardly Hall on his belly I straddled him and rooted both spurs onto his thighs he roared like a big calf attacked by dogs and shifted several yards of the fence I got his

(Page 10)

hands at the back of his neck and tried to make him let the revolver go but he stuck to it like grim death to a dead volunteer he called for assistance to a man named Cohen and Barnett, Lewis, Thompson, Jewitt two blacksmiths who was looking on I dare not strike any of them as I was bound to keep the peace or I could have spread those curs like dung in a paddock.

they got ropes tied my hands and feet and Hall beat me over the head with his six chambered colts revolver nine stitches were put in some of the cuts by Dr Hastings And when Wild Wright and my mother came they could trace us across the street by the blood in the dust and which spoiled the lustre of the paint on the gate-post of the Barracks Hall sent for more Police and Doctor Hastings Next morning I was handcuffed

(Page 11)

a rope tied from them to my legs and to the seat of the cart and taken to Wangaratta Hall was frightened I would throw him out of the cart so he tied me whilst Constable Arthur laughed at his cowardice for it was he who escorted me and Hall to Wangaratta. I was tried and committed as Hall swore I claimed the mare the Doctor died or he would have proved Hall a perjurer Hall has been tried several times for perjury but got clear as this is no crime in the Police force it is a credit to a Policeman to convict an innocent man but any muff can pot a guilty one Halls character is well known about El Dorado and Snowy Creek and Hall was considerably in debt to Mr L. O'Brien and he was going

(Page 12)

to leave Greta Mr O'Brien seen no other chance of getting his money so there was a subscription collected for Hall and with the aid of this money he got James Murdock who was recently hung in Wagga Wagga to give false evidence against me but I was acquitted on the charge of horsestealing and on Halls and Murdocks evidence I was found guilty of receiving and got 3 years experience in Beechworth Pentridges dungeons. this is the only charge ever proved against me Therefore I can say I never was convicted of horse or cattle stealing. My Brother Dan was never charged with assaulting a woman but he was sentenced to three months without the option of a fine and one month and two pound fine

(Page 13)

for damaging property by Mr Butler P.M. a sentence that there is no law to uphold therefore the minister of Justice neglected his duty in that case, but there never was such a thing as justice in the English laws but any amount of injustice to be had. Out of over thirty head of the very best horses the land could produce I could only find one when I got my liberty. Constable Flood stole and sold the most of them to the navvies on the railway line one bay cob he stole and sold four different times the line was completed and the men all gone when I came out and Flood was shifted to Oxley. he carried on the same game there all the stray horses that was any time without an owner and not in the Police Gazette Flood used to claim

(Page 14)

He was doing a good trade at Oxley until Mr Brown of the Laceby Station got him shifted as he was always running his horses about. Flood is different to Sergeant Steel, Strachan, Hall and the most of Police a[s] they have got to hire cads and if they fail the police are quite helpless. But Flood can make a cheque singlehanded he is the greatest horsestealer with the exception of myself and George King I know of. I never worked on a farm a horse and saddle was never traced to me after leaving employment since February 1873 I worked as a faller at Mr J. Saunders and R Rules sawmills then for Heach and Dockendorf I never worked for less than two pound ten a week since I left Pentridge

(Page 15)

and in 1875 or 1876 I was overseer for Saunders and Rule. Bourkes waterholes sawmills in Victoria since then I was on the King river, during my stay there I ran in a wild bull which I gave to Lydicher a farmer he sold him to Carr a Publican and Butcher who killed him for beef, sometime afterwards I was blamed for stealing this bull from James Whitty Boggy Creek I asked Whitty Oxley racecourse why he blamed me for stealing his bull he said he had found his bull and never blamed me but his son-in-law Farrell told him he heard I sold the bull to Carr not long afterwards I heard again I was blamed for stealing a mob of calves from Whitty and Farrell which I knew nothing about. I began to think they wanted

(Page 16)

me to give them something to talk about. Therefore I started wholesale and retail horse and cattle dealing Whitty and Burns not being satisfied with all the picked land on the Boggy Creek and King River and the run of their stock on the certificate ground free and no one interfering with

them paid heavy rent to the banks for all the open ground so as a poor
man could keep no stock, and impounded every beast they could get,
even off Government roads. If a poor man happened to leave his horse
or a bit of a poddy calf outside his paddock they would be impounded.
I have known over 60 head of horses impounded in one day by Whitty
and Burns all belonging to poor farmers they would have to leave their

(Page 17)

ploughing or harvest or other employment to go to Oxley. When they
would get there perhaps not have money enough to release them and
have to gave a bill of sale or borrow the money which is no easy matter.
And along with this sort of work, Farrell the Policeman stole a horse
from George King and had him in Whitty and Farrell's Paddocks until
he left the force and all this was the cause of me and my stepfather
George King taking their horses and selling them to Baumgarten and
Kennedy. the pick of them was taken to a good market and the culls
were kept in Petersons paddock and their brands altered by me two
was sold to Kennedy and the rest to Baumgarten who were strangers
to me and I believe honest men.

(Page 18)

They paid me full value for the horses and could not have known
they were stolen. no person had anything to do with the stealing and
selling of the horses but me and George King.

William Cooke who was convicted for Whitty's horses was innocent
he was not in my company at Petersons. But it is not the place of the
Police to convict guilty men as it is by them they get their living had
the right parties been convicted it would have been a bad job for the
Police as Berry would have sacked a great many of them only I came
to their aid and kept them in their bilits and good employment and
got them double pay and yet the ungrateful articles convicted my
mother and an infant my brother-in-law and another man

(Page 19)

who was innocent and still annoy my brothers and sisters and the
ignorant unicorns even threaten to shoot myself But as soon as I am
dead they will be heels up in the muroo. there will be no more police

required they will be sacked and supplanted by soldiers on low pay in the towns and special constables made of some of the farmers to make up for this double pay and expence. It will pay Government to give those people who are suffering innocence, justice and liberty. if not I will be compelled to show some colonial strategm which will open the eyes of not only the Victoria Police and inhabitants but also the whole British army and now doubt they will acknowledge their hounds were barking at the

(Page 20)

wrong stump and that Fitzpatrick will be the cause of greater slaughter to the Union Jack than Saint Patrick was to the snakes and toads in Ireland. The Queen of England was as guilty as Baumgarten and Kennedy Williamson and Skillion of what they were convicted for When the horses were found on the Murray River I wrote a letter to Mr Swanhill of Lake Rowan to acquaint the Auctioneer and to advertize my horses for sale I brought some of them to that place but did not sell I sold some of them in Benalla Melbourne and other places and left the colony and became a rambling gambler soon after I left there was a warrant for me and the Police searched the place and watched

(Page 21)

night and day for two or three weeks and when they could not snare me they got a warrant against my brother Dan And on the 15th of April Fitzpatrick came to the eleven mile creek to arrest him he had some conversation with a horse dealer whom he swore was William Skillion this man was not called in Beechworth, besides several other witnesses, who alone could have proved Fitzpatricks falsehood after leaving this man he went to the house asked was Dan in Dan came out. I hear previous to this Fitzpatrick had some conversation with Williamson on the hill. he asked Dan to come to Greta with him as he had a warrant for him for stealing

(Page 22)

Whitty's horses Dan said all right they both went inside Dan was having something to eat his mother asked Fitzpatrick what he wanted Dan for. the trooper said he had a warrant for him Dan then asked him to produce it he said it was only a telegram sent from Chiltern but Sergeant Whelan ordered him to releive Steel at Greta and call and arrest Dan and take him into Wangaratta next morning and get him remanded Dans mother said Dan need not go without a warrant unless he liked and that the trooper had no business on her premises without some authority besides his own word The trooper pulled out his

(Page 23)

revolver and said he would blow her brains out if she interfered. in the arrest she told him it was a good job for him Ned was not there or he would ram the revolver down his throat Dan looked out and said Ned is coming now, the trooper being off his guard looked out and when Dan got his attention drawn he dropped the knife and fork which showed he had no murderous intent and slapped heenan's hug on him took his revolver and kept him there until Skillion and Ryan came with horses which Dan sold that night. The trooper left and invented some scheme to say that he got shot which any man can see is false, he told Dan to

(Page 24)

clear out that Sergeant Steel and Detective Brown and Strachan would be there before morning Strachan had been over the Murray trying to get up a case against him and they would convict him if they caught him as the stock society offored an enticement for witnesses to swear anything and the germans over the Murray would swear to the wrong man as well as the right. Next day Williamson and my mother was arrested and Skillion the day after who was not there at all at the time of the row which can be proved by 8 or 9 witnesses And the Police got great credit and praise in the papers for arresting the mother of 12 children one an infant on her breast and those two quiet

(Page 25)

hard working innocent men who would not know the difference a revolver and a saucepan handle and kept them six months awaiting trial and then convicted them on the evidence of the meanest article that ever the sun shone on it seems that the jury was well chosen by the Police as there was a discharged Sergeant amongst them which is contrary to law they thought it impossible for a Policeman to swear a lie but I can assure them it is by that means and hiring cads they get promoted I have heard from a trooper that he never knew Fitzpatrick to be one night sober and that he sold his sister to a chinaman but he looks a young strapping rather genteel more fit to be a

(Page 26)

starcher to a laundress than a Policeman. For to a keen observer he has the wrong appearance for a manly heart the deceit and cowardice is too plain to be seen in the puny cabbage hearted looking face. I heard nothing of this transaction until very close on the trial I being then over 400 miles from Greta when I heard I was outlawed and a hundred pound reward for me for shooting a trooper in Victoria and a hundred pound for any man that could prove a conviction of horsestealing against me so I came back to Victoria knew I would get no justice if I gave myself up I enquired after my brother Dan and found him digging on Bullock Creek heard how the Police

(Page 27)

used to be blowing that they would not ask me to stand they would shoot me first and then cry surrender and how they used to rush into the house upset all the milk dishes break tins of eggs empty the flour out of bags onto the ground and even the meat out of the cask and destroy all the provisions and shove the girls in front of them into the rooms like dogs so as if anyone was there they would shoot the girls first but they knew well I was not there or I would have scattered their blood and brains like rain I would manure the Eleven Mile with their bloated carcasses and yet remember there is not one drop of murderous blood in my Veins.

(Page 28)

Superintendent Smith used to say to my sisters see all the men I have out today I will have as many more tomorrow and we will blow him into pieces as small as paper that is in our guns Detective Ward and Constable Hayes took out their revolvers and threatened to shoot the girls and children in Mrs Skillions absence the greatest ruffians and murderers no matter how deprived would not be guilty of such a cowardly action, and this sort of cruelty and disgraceful and cowardly conduct to my brothers and sisters who had no protection coupled with the conviction of my mother and those men certainly made my blood boil as I don't think there is a man born could have

(Page 29)

the patience to suffer it as long as I did or ever allow his blood to get cold while such insults as these were unavenged and yet in every paper that is printed I am called the blackest and coldest blooded murderer ever on record But if I hear any more of it I will not exactly show them what cold blooded murder is but wholesale and retail slaughter something different to shooting three troopers in self defence and robbing a bank. I would have been rather hot blooded to throw down my rifle and let them shoot me and my innocent brother, they were not satisfied with frightening my sisters night and day and destroying their provisions and lagging my mother and infant

(Page 30)

and those innocent men but should follow me and my brother into the wilds where he had been quietly digging neither molesting or inter-fering with anyone he was making good wages as the creek is very rich within half a mile from where I shot Kennedy. I was not there long and on the 25th of October I came on Police tracks between Table top and the bogs. I crossed them and returning in the evening I came on a different lot of tracks making for the shingle hut I went to our camp and told my brother and his two mates me and my brother went and found their camp at the shingle hut about a mile from my brothers house. We saw they carried long

(Page 31)

firearms and we knew our doom was sealed if we could not beat those before the others would come as I knew the other party of Police would soon join them and if they came on us at our camp they would shoot us down like dogs at our work as we had only two guns we thought it best to try and bail those up, take their firearms and ammunition and horses and we could stand a chance with the rest We approached the spring as close as we could get to the camp as the intervening space being clear ground and no battery We saw two men at the logs they

got up and one took a double barreled fowling-piece and fetched a
horse down and hobbled him at the tent

(Page 32)

we thought there were more men in the tent asleep those outside
being on sentry we could have shot those two men without speaking
but not wishing to take their lives we waited McIntyre laid the gun
against a stump and Lonigan sat on the log I advanced, my brother
Dan keepin[g] McIntyre covered which he took to be Constable
Flood and had he not obeyed my orders, or at-tempted to reach for
the gun or draw his revolver he would have been shot dead but when
I called on them to throw up their hands McIntyre obeyed and
Lonigan ran some six or seven yards to a battery of logs insted of
dropping behind the one he was sitting on, he had just got to the logs
and put

(Page 33)

his head up to take aim when I shot him that instant or he would
have shot me as I took him to be Strachan the man who said he
would not ask me to stand he would shoot me first like a dog. But it
happened to be Lonigan the man who in company with Sergeant
Whelan Fitzpatrick and King the Bootmaker and Constable ODay
that tried to put a pair of hand-cuffs on me in Benalla but could not
and had to allow McInnis the miller to put them on, previous to
Fitzpatrick swear-ing he was shot, I was fined two pounds for hitting
Fitzpatrick and two pounds for not allowing five curs like Sergeant
Whelan O.Day Fitz-patrick King and Lonigan who caught me by the
privates

(Page 34)

and would have sent me to Kingdom come only I was not ready and
he is the man that blowed before he left Violet Town if Ned Kelly was
to be shot he was the man would shoot him and no doubt he would
shoot me even if I threw up my arms and laid down as he knew four
of them could not arrest me single handed not to talk of the rest of
my mates, also either me or him would have to die, this he knew well
therefore he had a right to keep out of my road, Fitzpatrick is the

only one I hit out of the five in Benalla this shows my feeling towards
him as he said we were good friends & even swore it but he was the
biggest enemy I had in the country with the exception

(Page 35)

of Lonigan and he can be thankful I was not there when he took a
revolver and threatened to shoot my mother in her own house it is
not [true I fired] three shots and miss him at a yard and a half I don't
think I would use a revolver to shoot a man like him when I was
within a yard and a half of him or attempt to fire into a house where
my mother brothers and sisters was. and according to Fitzpatricks
statement all around him a man that is such a bad shot as to miss a
man three times at a yard and a half would never attempt to fire into
a house among a house full of women and children while I had a pairs
of arms and bunch of fives on the end of them

(Page 36)

That never failed to peg out anything they came in contact with
and Fitzpatrick knew the weight of one of them only too well, as it
run against him once in Benalla, and cost me two pound odd as he is
very subject to fainting. As soon as I shot Lonigan he jumped up and
staggered some distance from the logs with his hands raised and then
fell he surrendered but too late I asked McIntyre who was in the tent
he replied no one. I advanced and took possession of their two revolvers
and fowling-piece which I loaded with bullets instead of shot. I asked
McIntyre where his mates was he said they had gone down the creek
and he did not expect them that night he asked me was I

(Page 37)

going to shoot him and his mates. I told him no. I would shoot no
man if he gave up his arms and leave the force he said the police all
knew Fitzpatrick had wronged us. and he intended to leave the force,
as he had bad health, and his life was insured, he told me he intended
going home and that Kennedy and Scanlan were out looking for our
camp and also about the other Police he told me the N.S.W. Police
had shot a man for shooting Sergeant Walling I told him if they did,
they had shot the wrong man And I expect your gang came to do the

same with me he said no they did not come to shoot me they came to apprehend me I asked him what they carried spencer rifles and breech loading fowling pieces and so much ammunition for as the Police was

(Page 38)

only supposed to carry one revolver and 6 cartridges in the revolver but they had eighteen rounds of revolver cartridges each three dozen for the fowling piece and twenty one spenceir rifle cartridges and God knows how many they had away with the rifle this looked as if they meant not only to shoot me only to riddle me but I dont know either Kennedy Scanlan or him and had nothing against them, he said he would get them to give up their arms if I would not shoot them as I could not blame them, they had to do their duty I said I did not blame them for doing honest duty but I could not suffer them blowing me to pieces in my own native land and they knew Fitzpatrick wronged

(Page 39)

us and why not make it public and convict him but no they would rather riddle poor unfortunate creoles. but they will rue the day ever Fitzpatrick got among them Our two mates came over when they heard the shot fired but went back again for fear the Police might come to our camp while we were all away and manure bullock flat with us on our arrival. I stopped at the logs and Dan went back to the spring for fear the troopers would come in that way but I soon heard them coming up the creek. I told McIntyre to tell them to give up their arms, he spoke to Kennedy who was some distance in front of Scanlan he reached for his revolver and jumped off, on the off

(Page 40)

side of his horse and got behind a tree when I called on them to throw up their arms and Scanlan who carried the rifle slewed his horse around to gallop away but the horse would not go and as quick as thought fired at me with the rifle without unslinging it and was in the act of firing again when I had to shoot him and he fell from his horse.

I could have shot them without speaking but their lives was no good to me. McIntyre jumped on Kennedys horse and I allowed him to go as I did not like to shoot him after he surrendered or I would have

shot him as he was between me and Kennedy therefore I could not
shoot Kennedy without shooting him first. Kennedy kept firing from

(Page 41)

behind the tree my brother Dan advanced and Kennedy ran I followed
him he stopped behind another tree and fired again. I shot him in the
arm pit and he dropped his revolver and ran I fired again with the gun
as he slewed around to surrender I did not know he had dropped his
revolver the bullet passed through the right side of his chest & he could
not live or I would have let him go had they been my own brothers I
could not help shooting there or else let them shoot me which they
would have done had their bullets been directed as they intended them.
But as for handcuffing Kennedy to a tree or cutting his ear off or
brutally treating any of them, is a falsehood, if Kennedys ear was cut
off it was not done by me and none

(Page 42)

of my mates was near him after he was shot I put his cloak over him
and left him as well as I could and were they my own brothers I could
not have been more sorry for them this cannot be called wilful murder
for I was compelled to shoot them, or lie down and let them shoot me
it would not be wilful murder if they packed our remains in, shattered
into a mass of animated gore to Mansfield, they would have got great
praise and credit as well as promotion but I am reconed a horrid brute
because I had not been cowardly enough to lie down for them under
such trying circumstances and insults to my people certainly their wives
and children are to be pitied but they must remember those men came
into the bush with the intention

(Page 43)

of scattering pieces of me and my brother all over the bush and yet they
know and acknowledge I have been wronged and my mother and four
or five men lagged innocent and is my brothers and sisters and my
mother not to be pitied also who has no alternative only to put up with
the brutal and cowardly conduct of a parcel of big ugly fat-necked
wombat headed big bellied magpie legged narrow hipped splaw-footed
sons of Irish Bailiffs or english landlords which is better known as

Officers of Justice or Victorian Police who some calls honest gentlemen but I would like to know what business an honest man would have in the Police as it is an old saying It takes a rogue to catch a rogue and a

(Page 44)

man that knows nothing about roguery would never enter the force an take an oath to arrest brother sister father or mother if required and to have a case and conviction if possible Any man knows it is possible to swear a lie and if a policeman looses a conviction for the sake of swearing a lie he has broke his oath therefore he is a perjuror either ways. A Policeman is a disgrace to his country, not alone to the mother that suckled him, in the first place he is a rogue in his heart but too cowardly to follow it up without having the force to disguise it. next he is a traitor to his country ancestors and religion as they were all catholics before the Saxons and Cranmore yoke held sway since then they were perse

(Page 45)

cuted massacred thrown into martyrdom and tortured beyond the ideas of the present generation What would people say if they saw a strapping big lump of an Irishman shepherding sheep for fifteen bob a week or tailing turkeys in Tallarook ranges for a smile from Julia or even begging his tucker, they would say he ought to be ashamed of himself and tar-and-feather him. But he would be king to a policeman who for a lazy loafing cowardly bilit left the ash corner deserted the shamrock, the emblem of true wit and beauty to serve under a flag and nation that has destroyed massacreed and murdered their fore-fathers by the greatest of torture as rolling them down hill in spiked barrels

(Page 46)

pulling their toe and finger nails on the wheel. and every torture imaginable more was transported to Van Diemand's Land to pine their young lives away in starvation and misery among tyrants worse than the promised hell itself all of true blood bone and beauty, that was not murdered on their own soil, or had fled to America or other countries to bloom again another day, were doomed to Port Mcquarie Toweringabbie norfolk island and Emu plains in those places of tyranny

and condemnation many a blooming Irishman rather than subdue to
the Saxon yoke Were flogged to death and bravely died in servile chains
but true to the shamrock and a credit to Paddys land What would
people say if I became a policeman and took

(Page 47)

an oath to arrest my brothers and sisters and relations and convict
them by fair or foul means after the conviction of my mother and the
persecutions and insults offered to myself and people Would they say
I was a decent gentleman, and yet a police-man is still in worse and
guilty of meaner actions than that The Queen must surely be proud
of such heroic men as the Police and Irish soldiers as It takes eight or
eleven of the biggest mud crushers in Melbourne to take one poor
little half starved larrakin to a watchhouse. I have seen as many as
eleven, big & ugly enough to lift Mount Macedon out of a crab hole
more like the species of a baboon or Guerilla than a man

(Page 48)

actually come into a court house and swear they could not arrest one
eight stone larrakin and them armed with battens and niddies without
some civilians assistance and some of them going to the hospital from
the effects of hits from the fists of the larrakin and the Magistrate would
send the poor little Larrakin into a dungeon for being a better man
than such a parcel of armed curs. What would England do if America
declared war and hoisted a green flag as its all Irishman that has got
command of her armies forts and batteries even her very life guards
and beef tasters are Irish would they not slew around and fight her
with their own arms for the sake of the colour they dare not wear

(Page 49)

for years. and to reinstate it and rise old Erins isle once more from the
pressure and tyrannism of the English yoke, which has kept it in poverty
and starvation and caused them to wear the enemys coats. What else can
England expect. Is there not big fat-necked Unicorns enough paid to
torment and drive me to do thing[s] which I dont wish to do, without
the public assisting them I have never interfered with any person unless
they deserved it, and yet there are civilians who take firearms against me,

for what reas-on I do not know, unless they want me to turn on them and extermin-ate them without medicine. I shall be compelled to make an example of some of them if they cannot find no other employment

(Page 50)

If I had robbed and plundered ravished and murdered everything I met young and old rich and poor, the public could not do any more than take firearms and Assisting the police as they have done, but by the light that shines pegged on an ant-bed with their bellies opened their fat taken out rendered and poured down their throat boiling hot will be [c]ool to what pleasure I will give some of them and any person aiding or harbouring or assisting the Police in any way whatever or employing any person whom they know to be a detective or cad or those who would be so deprived as to take blood money will be outlawed and declared unfit to be allowed human buriel their property

(Page 51)

either consumed or confiscated and them theirs and all belonging to them exterminated off the face of the earth, the enemy I cannot catch myself I shall give a payable reward for, I would like to know who put that article that reminds me of a poodle dog half clipped in the lion fashion, called Brooke E. Smith Superin-tendent of Police he knows as much about commanding Police as Cap-tain Standish does about mustering mosquitoes and boiling them down for their fat on the back blocks of the Lachlan for he has a head like a turnip a stiff neck as big as his shoulders narrow hipped and pointed towards the feet like a vine stake and if there is any one to be called a murderer

(Page 52)

regarding Kennedy, Scanlan and Lonigan it is that mis-placed poodle he gets as much pay as a dozen good troopers, if there is any good in them, and what does he do for it he cannot look behind him without turning his whole frame it takes three or four police to keep sentry while he sleeps in Wangaratta, for fear of body snatchers do they think he is a superior animal to the men that has to guard him if so why not send the men that gets big pay and reconed superior to the common police after me and you shall soon save the country of high salaries to

men that is fit for nothing else but getting better men than him self
shot and sending orphan children to the industrial school

(Page 53)

to make prostitutes and cads of them for the Detectives and other evil
dis-posed persons Send the high paid and men and that received big
salaries for years in a gang by themselves after me, As it makes no
difference to them but it will give them a chance of showing whether
they are worth more pay than a common trooper or not and I think
the Public will soon find they are only in the road of good men and
obtaining money under false pretences, I do not call McIntyre a coward
for I reckon he is as game a man as wears the jacket as he had the
presence of mind to know his position, directly as he was spoken to,
and only foolishness to disobey, it was cowardice that made Lonigan
and the others fight it is only

(Page 54)

foolhardiness to disobey an outlaw as any Police-man or other man
who do not throw up their arms directly as I call on them knows the
consequences which is a speedy dispatch to Kingdom Come, I wish
those men who joined the stock protection society to with-draw their
money and give it and as much more to the widows and orphans and
poor of Greta district where I spent and will again spend many a
happy day fearless free and bold as it [the money] only aids the police
to procure false witnesses and go whacks with men to steal horses and
lag innocent men it would suit them far better to subscribe a sum and
give it to the poor of the district and there is no fear of anyone stealing
their property for no man

(Page 55)

could steal their horses without the knowledge of the poor if any man
was mean enough to steal their property the poor would rise out to a
man and find them if they were on the face of the earth it will always
pay a rich man to be liberal with the poor and make as little enemies
as he can as he shall find if the poor is on his side he shall loose nothing
by it, If they depend in the police they shall be drove to destruction,
As they can not and will not protect them if duffing and bushranging

were abolished the police would have to cadge for their living I speak
from experience as I have sold horses and cattle innumerable and yet
eight head of the culls is all ever was found I never was interfered with
whilst I kept up this successful

(Page 56)

trade. I give fair warning to all those who has reason to fear me to sell
out and give £10 out of every hundred towards the widow and orphan
fund and do not attempt to reside in Victoria but as short a time as
possible after reading this notice, neglect this and abide by the
consequences, which shall be worse than the rust in the wheat in
Victoria or the druth of a dry season to the grasshoppers in New
South Wales I do not wish to give the order full force without giving
timely warning. but I am a widows son outlawed and my orders must
be obeyed.

EDWARD KELLY[6]

Despite its importance, the Jerilderie Letter has rarely received the
attention it deserves. Like other expressions of popular discontent and
sympathy for the Kellys it is usually relegated to an appendix, when it
is printed at all. This kind of approach undermines the work of most
writers who have proclaimed their intention of explaining the popular
view of the Kelly phenomenon. That view cannot be fully compre-
hended without reference to the expressions of those people who supported or sympathised with the bushrangers. As the unofficial culture
of a period is rarely preserved in any retrievable form, particularly when
it involves illegal activity, we have to listen to the songs and poetry made
by Kelly sympathisers during and after the outbreak and, where possible, to the words of the participants themselves. The Jerilderie Letter
gives us a rare opportunity to do just that.

Often said to have been written by at least three different writers,[7]
the Jerilderie Letter is now known to be in Joe Byrne's hand. It is mainly
concerned to explain and justify Ned Kelly's actions since the age of
about sixteen. He called it 'a bit of my life'.[8]

Beginning with the farcical events of 1869 that led him to see the
inside of Beechworth gaol for the first time, Ned catalogues the injus-

tices and persecutions endured by himself and the family. In 1878 one
of the run-of-the-mill confrontations between the Kellys and the
police rapidly escalated into the outbreak after the imprisonment of
Mrs Kelly. As Ned Kelly explains these events they constitute a classic
case of an individual being forced into outlawry simply because he
attempts to defend himself and his family from the unjust actions of
the authorities. There is no doubt that the majority of selectors and bush
workers in north-eastern Victoria interpreted these events in exactly
the same manner.

This sympathy was maintained when the gang shot the three policemen at Stringybark Creek in what the press and the force characterised
as cold-blooded murder. The totally opposite reaction of Kelly sympathisers has already been seen in the song 'Stringybark Creek', written
immediately after the event. In the Jerilderie Letter Ned Kelly describes
the battle as self-defence, maintaining, probably truthfully,[9] that the
bushrangers only fired after the police had fired on them. Ned also says
that the police had it coming to them anyway for their past injustices,
to others as well as the Kellys.

This is more than the attempt of a murderer to explain his actions.
Kelly is justifying his actions in terms of the highwayman tradition as
the righteous revenge of the oppressed against their oppressors. Ned
Kelly and his friends hated the police as the coercive tools of the squatters and the government. This was linked with the Kellys' view that
the Victorian police were traitors to the cause of Irish nationalism,
having taken service with the English Crown.

There are a number of anti-English outbursts in the Jerilderie Letter,
these being the main additions to the earlier Cameron Letter which
served as a model for the Jerilderie Letter. In one remarkable passage,
Ned Kelly attains the heights of oral re-creation and the zenith of his
denigration of the police. Given that Ned Kelly could not write[10] and
that the original letter was written in different hands, it is probable
that one section at least of the letter is an oral reworking of a traditional
Australian convict song. 'Moreton Bay', or 'The Convict's Lament',
is a rather grim account of penal life, probably composed around 1830
by one 'Frank the Poet', or Francis MacNamara, and transmitted orally
since then. One verse of the song goes like this:

> He said, I have been a prisoner at Port Macquarie,
>   at Norfolk Island and Emu Plains,
> At Castle Hill and cursed Towngabbie — at all those
>   places I've worked in chains;
> But of all the places of condemnation in each penal
>   station of New South Wales,
> Moreton Bay I found no equal, for excessive tyranny
>   each day prevails.[11]

Compare this with the following lines from the Jerilderie Letter, describing the fate of Irish convicts in Australia:

> . . . [they] were doomed to Port McQuarie Toweringabbie Norfolk island and Emu plains and in those places of tyranny and condemnation many a blooming Irishman rather than subdue to the Saxon yoke were flogged to death and bravely died in servile chains . . .[12]

Obviously Ned Kelly was familiar with the song 'Moreton Bay', which describes the sufferings of a transported Irishman, and his anticipated release from 'tyranny' when his cruel gaoler, Captain Logan, is murdered by an Aboriginal. It was a significant theme for the bushranger to recall during his impassioned recrimination of north-eastern Victorian society. The passage also shows that Ned was familiar with the bitter underground traditions stretching back to the penal years and beyond them to the long agonies of Ireland's struggle against England. It was only through such oral traditions that the Kellys were able to articulate and activate their discontent. Poorly educated, poorly represented in Parliament, and just plain poor, the Kellys, and many like them, had no other means of expressing their anger than through the inherited images and clichés of Irish nationalism.

Yet the Kellys were not actually motivated by such sentiments. It was the immediate north-eastern Victorian tensions and conflicts that led to the outbreak, not a mis-begotten dream of creating an Hibernian utopia in the Wombat Ranges, as implied by some writers. The police, the government, and the squatters' practice of impounding stray stock

are the main complaints of the Jerilderie Letter and were the underly-
ing reasons for the outbreak itself.

Undoubtedly, many sympathisers who were Irish or of Irish descent
would have responded to Ned's expression of his personal and family discontents in these terms. But there were many Kelly supporters of other
ethnic origins who responded to the more generally accessible framework for agrarian protest provided by the highwayman tradition. This
set of moral guidelines for outlaws was a concept that Ned Kelly both
subscribed to and manipulated in his letters and speeches. An eyewitness
at Jerilderie summarised the bushranger's address to the people like this:

> . . . the outlaws had openly avowed their intention of not interfering
> in any way with private individuals, and had even posed as champions
> of the oppressed against the oppressors of the poor . . . Kelly himself,
> when robbing the bank-safe, denounced all financial institutions as
> 'slavers' and 'Poor-man crushers'. Besides all these boastings of what
> he was going to do for the poor and oppressed, he followed it up by
> not taking anything away but the bank money, the policeman's horse,
> and a saddle out of the saddler's shop.[13]

Ned Kelly' was well aware that in order to retain popular sympathy and
support he had to be seen to act in accordance with the rules of the highwayman tradition and to appear to be robbing the rich to benefit the
poor.

At the end of the Jerilderie Letter Ned elevated this Robin Hood
ideal, if not to the level of a political manifesto, at least to the proposal
of a Mafia-like alternative state-within-a-state, a regional protection
racket. The members of the Stock Protection Society, mainly wealthy
landowners, are admonished to give their funds to 'the widows and poor
of the Greta district' who would then no longer be forced to steal in order
to live and would reciprocate by ensuring that no one else stole the property of the rich. According to Ned, this redistribution of wealth would
result in more harmonious social relationships and put an end to the
causes of bushranging and duffing. In turn, this would reduce the police
force to 'cadging' for a living, their services being no longer required.

This sort of thinking indicates that Ned Kelly and his friends had
some very definite ideas about the desirable organisation of north-

CHAPTER 7

SOME COLONIAL STRATAGEM

he Greta mob was a group of bush larrikins that included Dan Kelly and Joe Byrne. This collection of 'flash' horse-borrowers wore their chinstraps beneath their noses to signify youthful defiance of convention and Mob solidarity. The Kelly gang had its origins in the Greta Mob and drew most of its principal supporters and sometime participants from the same ranks, including Tom Lloyd Jun., Isaiah 'Wild' Wright, and Aaron Sherritt, Joe Byrne's best mate.

Sherritt could have joined the bushrangers but stayed out of trouble, pretending to act as a police informant while misleading them about the gang's activities. This dangerous role of double agent earned Sherritt the suspicion of the Lloyds and Quinns and, finally, the distrust of the gang. A letter from Joe Byrne to Aaron Sherritt, written on 26 June 1879, indicates the development of this distrust and the internal dissension that wracked the Kelly, Quinn, and Lloyd families, as well as the gang:

Dear Aaron,
I write these few stolen lines to let you know I am still living. I'm not the least afraid of being captured, dear Aaron. Meet me, you and Jack, This side of Puzzle Ranges. Neddy and I have come to the conclusion to get you to join us. I was advised to turn traitor, but I said I would die at Ned's side first.

Dear Aaron, it is best for you to join us, Aaron. A short life and a jolly one. The Lloyds and Quinns want you shot, but I say no you are on our side. If it is nothing only the sake of your mother and sisters. We sent that bloody Hart to your place twice. Did my mother tell you the message that I left for you. I slept at home three days on the 24th May. Did Patsy [Joe's brother, Paddy] give you the booty I left for you. I intend to pay old Sunday Doig and old Mullane, O, that bloody snob, where is he? I will make a target of him. Meet me on next Thursday, you and Jack, and we will have another bank quite handy. I told Hart to call last Thursday evening. I would like to know if he obeyed us or not, If not, we will shoot him.

If you come on our tracks, close your puss. We know you were at Kate's several times. You had just gone one night as we came. We followed you four miles, but returned without success. If you do not meet me where I ask you, meet me under London you-know. I will riddle that bloody Mullane if I catch him. No more from the enforced outlaw, until I see yourself.

I remain

Yours truly

You Know[1]

Exactly one year to the day after Joe Byrne wrote this letter, Aaron Sherritt was sharing an evening meal with his new wife, her mother, and four policemen in his two-room slab hut near Beechworth. There was a knock at the back door from one of Sherritt's neighbours who said he had lost his way home. Sherritt opened the door to put his neighbour on the right track but Joe Byrne stepped out of the darkness instead, holding a gun. Without a word he pulled the trigger and blew Sherritt back into the hut, then fired a second shot into his friend's bleeding body before it hit the dirt floor.

Two of the four policemen stationed at the hut to 'protect' Sherritt dived under the bed in the adjoining room and the other two hid themselves each side of the door.

'The bastard will never put me away again,' Joe Byrne said to the dead man's widow and her mother. 'He would harm me if he could; he did his best.'[2]

After two hours of unsuccessfully challenging the policemen to come out and fight and a mock attempt to set the hut alight, Joe Byrne and Dan Kelly rode away south-west towards Glenrowan. The climax of the Kelly tragedy would be played out in this ramshackle whistle-stop in the heart of the Kelly country.

The bushrangers had finally decided Sherritt must be eliminated. He had always been on the outer fringes of the Kelly clan, partly because he was not a relative and partly because he was a Protestant, or at least not a Catholic: 'he said he was nothing,' according to his wife.[3] But his murder had another purpose. Ned Kelly thought that news of the killing would bring a train-load of police from Benalla to Wangaratta and Beechworth, straight through the Kelly country. He planned to sabotage the railway line at Glenrowan, wreck the train and pick off the survivors. This would provide the gang and their supporters with arms and leave the countryside vulnerable for miles around.

What the Kellys planned to do next is still a matter of dispute. Some say they merely intended to rob as many banks as possible; others that they hoped to establish a republic of north-eastern Victoria. Whatever their plans, a local schoolteacher named Thomas Curnow upset them and precipitated the final gun-battle at the Glenrowan Inn.

As Joe Byrne and Dan Kelly galloped away from Sherritt's body and four badly frightened policemen, Ned Kelly and Steve Hart woke the Glenrowan stationmaster, a gang of railway labourers and two plate-layers, forcing them to tear up a stretch of track along the embankment where the outlaws hoped to wreck the train. Later in the morning, those men were herded into the Widow Jones's Glenrowan Inn, a tin and timber affair on the opposite side of the railway line from the Glen-rowan station. By lunchtime Sunday there were almost sixty people held at the inn, and still the train had not come.

The bushrangers had expected the train carrying the police rein-forcements to reach Glenrowan by ten on Sunday morning. But the four policemen at Sherritt's hut were too terrified to take the news to Beechworth until more than twelve hours after Joe Byrne and Dan Kelly had departed. This, and the usual police inefficiency and indecision, meant that the special train did not leave Benalla until after one o'clock on Monday morning.

In the meantime, the Kellys and their prisoners amused themselves by holding a bush spree. Someone had a concertina, there was plenty to drink and, as one of the prisoners later testified, 'He did not treat us badly — not at all'. Party games and cards were played, a dance developed in which Ned participated, and the landlady's son sang, 'The Wild Colonial Boy' and one of the Kelly ballads.[4]

By ten o'clock the train had still not arrived and Ned, perhaps more relaxed than he should have been, allowed some of the prisoners to go home. One of them was Thomas Curnow who told Ned he was worried about his wife and family being alone at night. Curnow went home, got a lantern and began walking back along the railway line to warn the police of their danger.

Just before three o'clock on Monday morning, the bushrangers heard the pilot engine's whistle warning the following police train of danger ahead and knew their plan had failed. Buckling on the suits of armour, weighing nearly 100 pounds each, which they had fashioned from stolen and donated ploughshares in readiness for a possible final pitched battle, the four members of the Kelly gang took up their positions by the hotel as the police train drew into the Glenrowan station.

Ned Kelly stood in front of his companions shouting that he was made of iron and firing at the police. Superintendent Hare was mildly wounded in the first exchange of shots and Ned soon received four or five wounds. The police took cover behind trees and in a shallow ditch near the inn. Dan Kelly, Joe Byrne and Steve Hart retreated inside the hotel and Ned strolled through the police lines, firing at the police and apparently impervious to their bullets. He then faded into the dark surrounding bush.

Most of the prisoners had escaped from the hotel soon after the arrival of the police. Those who still remained managed to get to safety during a lull in the firing caused by the arrival of reinforcements from Wangaratta. But the only remaining woman prisoner, Mrs Reardon, carrying her baby, was driven back inside by a police volley. The same thing had happened when she had tried to escape with the other prisoners the first time.

Back inside the hotel Dan Kelly told Mrs Reardon to try again and if she was successful to inform the troopers that the bushrangers would co-operate in a cease-fire, giving the rest of the prisoners a chance to get away.[5]

For the third time Mrs Reardon, accompanied by her husband and family, made a break for safety, and for the third time the police fired upon her. Mr Reardon and the rest of the family were forced back to the hotel, one of his sons receiving a wound that would cripple him for life. Only Mrs Reardon and her baby made it to safety at the rear of the police cordon. She gave the police Dan Kelly's message but it went unheeded and they continued to rake the inn with gunfire.

Joe Byrne was killed as he stood at the bar toasting the bold Kelly gang. Police gunfire also wounded an old man and the young boy who had sung 'The Wild Colonial Boy' to Ned a few hours before. Both would die before the day's end. About this time, Ned Kelly walked effortlessly back through the police lines and into the hotel. He found Joe Byrne's body but could not locate Dan or Steve who were in one of the rear rooms. Assuming that they had escaped, he went out the back door of the hotel to make his own getaway only to discover that his horse had bolted. Ned Kelly then pierced the police lines yet again, finally fainting in the bush from loss of blood and exhaustion.

The siege continued with sporadic police gunfire, some of it directed at the bushrangers' horses to prevent any possible escape. The numerous armed sympathisers who gathered behind the station and watched from the SOME OF THE POLICE AT GLENROWAN. (POLICE MUSEUM, MELBOURNE)

bush did nothing. Perhaps Ned told them not to act, perhaps they could see that it was hopeless. No one knows. Just before dawn a calm descended on Glenrowan, as if everyone was waiting for something to happen.

Through the early morning mist a metallic ringing sound was heard and the newly revived Ned Kelly lumbered out of the bush like some bizarre robot blazing away at the police with a revolver. His wounds and the clumsiness of the armour ensured that Kelly did little more than frighten the police, some of whom thought the tall, macintosh-coated figure was the Bunyip, or even Old Nick. Ned was eventually brought down with a shotgun blast to the legs delivered by a Sergeant Steele who, with a Constable Dwyer, removed the fallen bushranger's helmet. On discovering that they had captured Ned Kelly, Dwyer kicked him and Steele was about to murder him in cold blood, when Constable Bracken reached the scene and threatened to shoot Steele himself if he tried to harm Kelly. The badly wounded outlaw was taken into custody at the Glenrowan railway station where he was made as comfortable as possible. He was not expected to live, and the last rites were given by Father Gibney, a passing Catholic priest.

PART OF THE AUDIENCE ON GLENROWAN RAILWAY STATION. (POLICE MUSEUM, MELBOURNE)

THE REMAINS OF THE
GLENROWAN INN. (POLICE
MUSEUM, MELBOURNE)

The police continued to fire upon the inn, which still contained prisoners, until 10 a.m. when the large crowd of spectators who had congregated on the railway station compelled Superintendent Sadleir to call a cease-fire and the prisoners were allowed to leave. Dan Kelly and Steve Hart attempted to escape after the release of the prisoners but were driven back to the hotel by the police.

When news of the Glenrowan showdown reached Melbourne the city virtually ground to a standstill, according to the *Australasian Sketcher*:

> Melbourne was a scene of unexampled excitement on June 28, in consequence of receipt of the news that the Kelly gang had been surrounded at Glenrowan. Business appeared to be suspended and the streets about the newspaper offices were blocked by excited crowds, eager for the latest intelligence from the scene of action . . . [6]

Requests for lights to illuminate the scene, should the siege continue into the night, and for a field gun to blow the inn apart, were telegraphed to Melbourne. Before any of these items arrived the police decided to

THE REMAINS OF DAN
KELLY OR STEVE HART.
(POLICE MUSEUM, MELBOURNE)

burn the hotel down at three that afternoon.

As the tinder-box building caught fire, Father Gibney rushed out of the crowd of onlookers, now five hundred strong, and into the hotel. He found Dan and Steve lying dead side by side, with no sign of bullet wounds or blood. He also found the badly wounded old man, Martin Cherry, who had been forgotten by the prisoners in their haste to escape. The police dragged the man out of the blaze, saving him from ending his life as a burned stump. He died shortly after.

An hour or so later, the charred remains of Dan Kelly and Steve Hart were dragged from the smouldering wreckage on sheets of tin and handed over to the relatives for mourning and burial. Joe Byrne's body, rescued intact from the building before the fire took hold, was taken to Benalla with Ned.

The next day the police decided that they should hold an inquest on the bodies of Dan and Steve, and strung the still handsome Joe Byrne up on the door of the Benalla Gaol for the interest of sightseers and the pecuniary motives of a local photographer who made his photographs into postcards and sold them throughout the colony.

News of the proposed inquest on the bushrangers' bodies provoked threats and rumours of impending violence from Kelly sympathisers. The police nervously cancelled the order and requested further police patrols in the disaffected north-east.

Being in excellent health, Ned Kelly once again refused to do what was expected of him and remained alive. He was taken to Melbourne the day after the siege and soon nursed back to health to stand trial. He was moved secretly to Beechworth gaol on 1 August for his hearing

THE MEDIA. (POLICE MUSEUM, MELBOURNE)

BOTTOM: JOE BYRNE'S BODY TIED TO THE DOOR OF THE BENALLA GAOL. THIS PHOTOGRAPH WAS SOLD AS A POSTCARD. (POLICE MUSEUM, MELBOURNE)

before the Bench of the Court of Petty Sessions which took place five days later. From there Ned Kelly was remanded to stand trial for the murders of Lonigan and Scanlon at the Melbourne City Court.

The mood of the Kelly country was black and tense. The feuds between sympathisers and police continued, though in a more clandestine manner. Jim Kelly's return from a five-year gaol term in New South Wales also worried the authorities, as did letters like these, written to the judge who was at first expected to preside over Ned Kelly's trial. The original spelling and punctuation have been retained:

THE ARMOUR. (POLICE MUSEUM, MELBOURNE)

Banyena
Sept. 8

To His Excellency Judge Cope

Sir,
I hereby give you timely notice that if you pass the sentence of death
on Ned Kelly and he gets hanged, three other gangs already formed to
my knowledge just waiting to see what will be done and they vow ven-
gence on the police everyone they meet. They say they won't pass them
by like Ned Kelly did. There are fourteen in one gang and eighteen in
the other, They say it started in Mansfield but it wont end there. There
are hundreds of respectable people that never were sympathisers nor
never intended to be swears that they will have revenge. More than
three parts of Victoria have sympathy for Ned Kelly

Dear Sir,
I am sure it would be well worth while to spare Ned Kelly's life for I
am sure those other gangs will put the country for greater expense
than ever the Kellys did and not that alone but all the police that will
loose their lives, over it. The country will be in a terrible state. They

say they will have revenge for the fifty police setting fire to a house rather than face two boys to burn them, They say if ever they get holt of Johnstone that was this man that set fire to the Glenrowan Hotel they will roast him alive.

The people all say they [the police] would sacrifice one hundred innocent lives to capture two boys so if they turn out they will make it hot for them. The whole country has sympathy for Ned Kelly so if you hang him mostly every sole in the country will have a down on you even all the ladies in this part of the country is as willing to turn out for Ned as well as the men. I am sure that poor Ned Kelly was driven out if just look, as if as if was your own case. I am sure no one could blame them for shooting them three police. The Kelly's lives were as good as theirs any day if not better. So you ought to draw it mild when you are passing the sentence on Ned Kelly. For your own sake for by all account you stand in danger. So hoping you see and understand the reason ableness of my letter.

I remain yours truly.

A. Lady[7]

But it was the same judge who had sentenced Mrs Kelly to a three-year sentence over the Fitzpatrick affair and thereby precipitated the outbreak who presided at her son's trial on 28 and 29 October 1880. Judge Redmond Barry directed the jury to consider a verdict of murder rather than manslaughter in the case of Edward Kelly. The jury took only half an hour to find the bushranger guilty. This dialogue then passed between Barry and the man he was about to condemn to death: 'Edward Kelly, the verdict is one which you must have fully expected.' Ned Kelly replied: 'Under the circumstances I did expect this verdict.' After some further words from the judge, the prisoner went on to say: 'I don't say this out of flashness, I do not recognise myself as a great man; but it is quite possible for me to clear myself of the charge if I liked to do so . . . I declare before you and my God that my mind is as easy and clear as it possibly can be.'

At this sensational statement there was uproar in the court. Banging his gavel, Barry snapped back at Kelly, 'It is blasphemous of you to say so.'

'I do not fear death,' Kelly said, and later on: 'I dare say the day will come when we shall all have to go to a bigger court than this. Then we will see who is right or who is wrong.'

Feeling obliged to answer this challenge, the judge said, 'An offence of the kind which you stand accused of is not of an ordinary character . . . A party of men took up arms against society, organised as it was for mutual protection and regard for the law.'

'Yes, that is the way the evidence brought it out,' interrupted Kelly.

'Unfortunately,' the judge continued, 'in a new community, where society was not bound together so closely as it should be, there was a class which looked upon the perpetrators of those crimes as heroes . . . It is remarkable that although New South Wales had joined Victoria in offering a large reward for the detection of the gang, no person was found to discover it. There seemed to be a spell cast over the people of this particular district, which I can only attribute either to sympathy with crime or dread of the consequences of doing their duty.'

After a further brief exchange, the Judge passed sentence of death, concluding with the usual, 'May the Lord have mercy on your soul.'

Ned Kelly said, 'Yes, I will meet you there.'[8] He was then removed from the court, though not from public prominence.

Ned Kelly was to be held in the condemned cell of Melbourne gaol until 10 a.m. on 11 November when he would pay for his crimes. In the meantime his energetic defence lawyer, David Gaunson, organised public meetings and petitions for Kelly's reprieve, obtaining 32,000 signatures, some gathered even in Jerilderie.[9]

'A Lady', though not the same one who had written to Judge Cope, wrote a pamphlet titled *Kelly's Defence*, and the call for reprieve showed signs of becoming a popular movement. But it was all to no avail. On Wednesday, 10 November, Ned saw his mother, brother Jim, and two of his sisters for the last time, had a photographic portrait made for the family and, according to tradition, heard his mother speak the famous words, 'Mind you die like a Kelly.' Next morning, Ned woke early and, according to tradition, was heard singing one of the Kelly songs, 'Farewell to My Home in Greta':

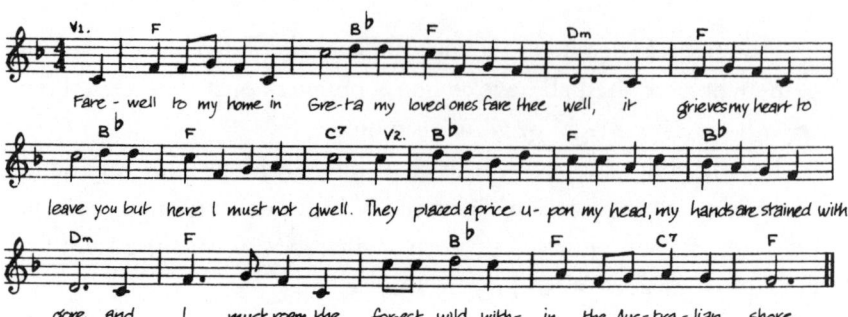

Fare-well to my home in Gre-ta my loved ones fare thee well, it grieves my heart to leave you but here I must not dwell. They placed a price u-pon my head, my hands are stained with gore, and I must roam the for-est wild with-in the Aus-tra-lian shore

But if they cross my cherished path,
By all I hold on earth
I'll give them cause to rue the day
Their mothers gave them birth.

I'll shoot them down like carrion crows
That roam our country wide,
And leave their bodies bleaching
Along some woodland side.

Oh Edward, darling brother
Surely you would not go
So rashly to encounter
With such a mighty foe.

Now don't you know that Sydney
And Melbourne are combined,
And for your apprehension, Ned
There are warrants duly signed.

To eastward lies great Bogong,
Towering to the sky
From east to west and then you'll find
That's Gippsland lying by.

You know the country well, Ned,
So take your comrades there,
And profit by your knowledge
Of the wombat and the bear.

NED KELLY, THE DAY BEFORE HIS
EXECUTION. A PORTRAIT TAKEN
FOR FAMILY AND FRIENDS. (POLICE
MUSEUM, MELBOURNE)

NED KELLY'S DEATH MASK. (INSTITUTE OF
ANATOMY, CANBERRA)

And let no childish quarrelling
Cause trouble in the gang;
You're up with one another,
And guard my brother Dan.

See, yonder ride four troopers,
One kiss before we part,
Now haste and join your comrades,
Dan, Joe Byrne and Stevey Hart.[10]

He received the last rites and walked steadily to the gallows, telling
the hangman that there was no need to tie his arms. On the scaffold
he sighed, 'Ah, well, I suppose it had to come to this.' Then the trap
was sprung.

Outside the prison a 4000-strong crowd of the 'lower orders' waited
relatively sedately. At ten o'clock there was a moment's silence: then
the crowd began to break up, having played their part in the ritual of
judicial death.

The body was cut down. Before burial within the walls of Melbourne gaol the head was severed for the casting of a death mask. A phrenologist also examined the skull and pronounced, without much fear of contradiction, that 'Ned Kelly was destined to a life of violence and crime which could only lead him to the scaffold'.

Ned Kelly had been hoisted into oblivion, his head severed, copied and 'scientifically' examined. Justice was seen to be done and Victoria could now continue to 'progress', letting the Kelly episode fade gradually into the colonial past.

But although the man was dead, his image lived on.

First of all, Ned Kelly's promise to Judge Barry that they would meet in the place of judgement, heavenly or otherwise, seemed to be prophetic. Five days after the execution Barry collapsed and, seven days later, died. The press was delighted and Ned's promise to the judge took on a new significance. Then there were the sittings of the Kelly Reward Board and the Royal Commission into the Police Force of Victoria. They dragged on through 1881, exposing the ineptitude and dissension within the force and keeping the public continually reminded of 'the Kelly business', as the Commissioners euphemistically called the outbreak.

All this contributed to the establishment of a ready market for popular 'Kellyana' in Victoria and elsewhere in the colonies. At the same time, the secret subterranean oral tradition, fired from the still-smouldering heart of the Kelly country, burned even more brightly than it had before.

CHAPTER 8

THE MAKING OF A HERO

I

f the Victorian authorities thought they had put an end to the 'Kelly business' by hanging the leader of the outbreak, they were badly mistaken. Popular interest in the bushranger did not slacken but began to express itself in both oral and media forms. Orally, the creation of Kelly folklore within the framework of the highwayman tradition continued, and songs, poems, legends and sayings proliferated.

Many of Ned Kelly's actions seemed tailor-made for the genesis of an Australian Robin Hood. Like many of his Australian predecessors he was well aware of the ethics required of a bushranger. To retain vital sympathy and support he and his companions had to act in the same manner as the outlaw heroes of traditional song and story. That meant not killing and plundering indiscriminately or without just cause, showing courtesy and generosity to women and the poor, and generally behaving in a manner appropriate to a ballad hero.

From the very first raid, Ned was at pains to ensure that things were done in proper highwayman style. Mrs Scott, wife of the Euroa bank manager, was greatly impressed by the outlaw's courtesy and manly bearing. 'Ned Kelly was a gentleman,' she stated on several occasions. No one seems to have been unduly interfered with by the gang, except Aaron Sherritt and he was the Judas who, in terms of the highwayman tradition, suffered a just and proper fate. Ned made Steve Hart return the watches he ungraciously tried to pocket at Jerilderie and also returned a horse he intended to 'borrow' for himself upon being told that it was the favourite mount of the publican's daughter. The gang always socialised with their captives, drank with them (at the bushrangers' own expense, it seems), danced, sang, and played party games with them, and generally gave everyone a roaring good time! That at least is the impression given by most of the eyewitness accounts of the Kelly raids. And, of course, Ned made public performances of burning the mortgages at Euroa and Jerilderie.

These apparently trivial acts were the stuff of Ned Kelly's popularity and continuing support. This was given a final and enduring boost by the public and violent nature of the events at Glenrowan, followed by Ned's trial and execution. A more suitable candidate for the image of the traditional outlaw hero would be difficult to come by. His early attainment of this mantle is evident from the publication of a number of Kelly songs while the outlaws were still active. As the editor of one of these compilations points out with pompous disapproval, the songs had an existence far beyond the pages upon which they were printed:

THE ROMANTIC MEDIA VIEW OF THE BUSH-RANGER. (*AUSTRALASIAN SKETCHER*, 31 JULY 1880)

> The widely extended and generally-expressed horror and detestation of the police murders which have been displayed through this colony, render more prominent the sympathy and admiration for the Kelly's, that by the larrikin class, are not only barely disguised in some cases, but openly vaunted in others.
>
> This is more noticeable amongst the youth in various large centres of population, where . . . they

congregate occasionally at street corners and elsewhere to sing ballads — hymns of triumph, as it were — in their praise. We have not been informed whether these lyrics have yet taken shape in print, but we have succeeded in obtaining the words of a few by taking them down from dictation.

They are, for the most part, wretched doggerel void of point as a rule, and in the metre — if metre it can be called — adapted to the universal Irish street-ballad tune . . .

The writer then went on to paint a ludicrous picture of the composer of these 'leprous distilments':

. . . we should imagine that the writer would find himself more at home in a 'thieves' kitchen' a St. Giles' ballad-mongery, or one of Her Majesty's jails, than at either a missionary meeting or the gathering together of a Young Men's Christian Association — unless, indeed, he attended with the intention of picking the pockets of the audience.[1]

CONTEMPORARY EVENTS.
(*AUSTRALASIAN SKETCHER*, 17 JULY 1880)

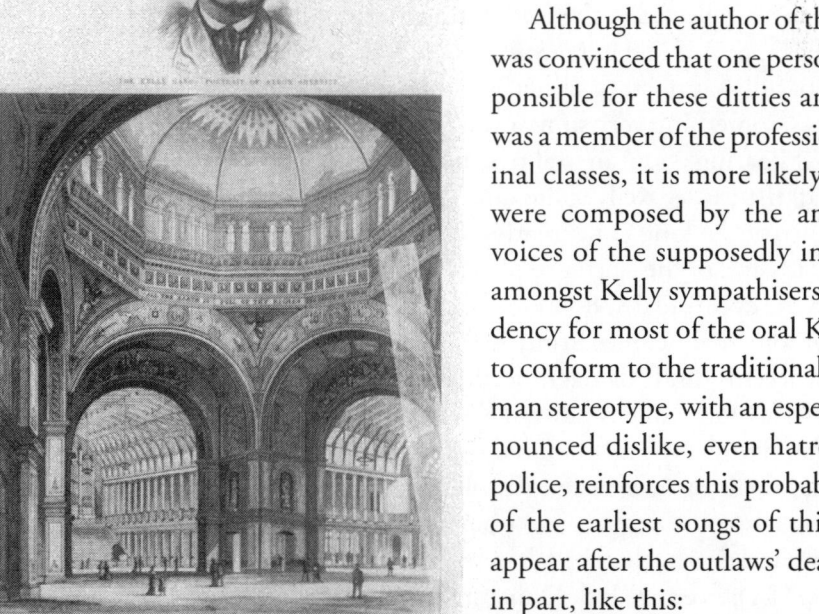

Although the author of these words was convinced that one person was responsible for these ditties and that he was a member of the professional criminal classes, it is more likely that they were composed by the anonymous voices of the supposedly inarticulate amongst Kelly sympathisers. The tendency for most of the oral Kelly songs to conform to the traditional highwayman stereotype, with an especially pronounced dislike, even hatred, of the police, reinforces this probability. One of the earliest songs of this kind to appear after the outlaws' deaths went, in part, like this:

FAREWELL DAN AND EDWARD KELLY

Dirty policemen did outdo you,
In a manner I am told;
Dirty policemen did outdo you
For that paltry sum of gold.

Thirty policemen did besiege you
In the hotel owned by Jones,
Then was our gallant leader
Nothing left you but the bones.

These verses are a hypothetical reconstruction of a song based on two oral versions collected in the field during the last thirty years and a fragment that appeared in the *Bulletin* in 1882. Like all such reconstructions it is not fully satisfactory, either as a song or as a social document. Nevertheless, something very similar was in existence as early as 1882 and was still floating about in oral tradition up to ninety years later.[2] Like most of the earlier Kelly songs already mentioned, this provides firm evidence of the long continuation of Ned Kelly's celebration in outlaw ballads and of the existence of a coherent oral tradition reaching back to the events of 1878–80.

Another song that belongs firmly within the oral tradition was collected quite recently and is a magnificently defiant example of the folk muse at its best. 'My Name is Edward Kelly' is a portrayal of the classic highwayman figure. Ned is honoured by his friends, fears no danger, and becomes an outlaw to avenge an insult to his sister. He shoots 'traps' (policemen), whom he despises as cowards, robs banks, and prefers to die ten thousand deaths than be taken by the government to hang on the gallows. His heroes are Jack Donahue and Ben Hall.

HEADLINE NEWS. (*AUSTRALASIAN SKETCHER*, 3 JULY 1880)

CURNOW WARNS THE POLICE TRAIN AT GLENROWAN. (*AUSTRALASIAN SKETCHER*, 31 JULY 1880)

HOW THE MEDIA SAW THE KELLYS AND THEIR FRIENDS. (*AUSTRALASIAN SKETCHER*, 17 JULY 1880)

THE TRIAL. (*AUSTRALASIAN SKETCHER*, 6 NOVEMBER 1880)

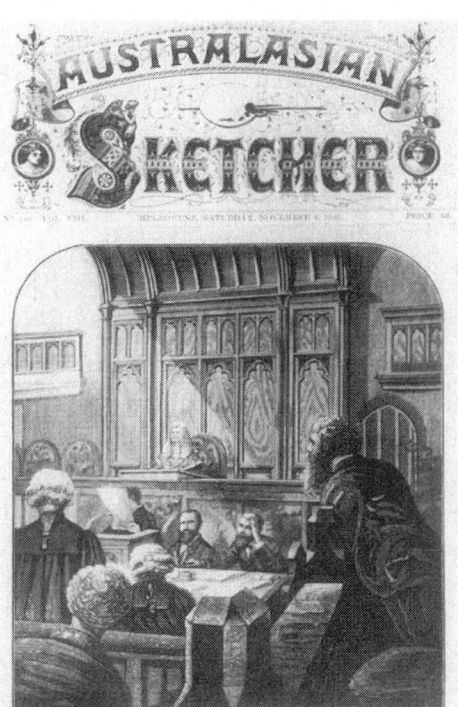

MY NAME IS EDWARD KELLY

My name is Ed-ward Kel-ly, I'm hon-oured vast-ly well. I
rule su-preme my word is law where-ev-er I may dwell. My
friends are all u-nit-ed, my mates and ar-my near; we
sleep be-neath some sha-dy tree, no dan-ger do we fear.

Now the first of my adventures was through my sister dear,
Who was grossly insulted and put in bodily fear;
And when I came to hear of this it made my poor heart ache;
I took to the hills to have revenge all for my sister's sake.

I am young and in my youthful days, I'm twenty-four years old.
I've spent some time in vanity among young girls so bold.
But now I am a-robbing, and loudly guns do roar.
'Twas there I shot poor Kennedy, which grieved my heart full sore.

In Mansfield that fair township where I was bred and born,
Oft-times have I roamed those hills from dark till early morn,
But now I am a-robbing upon the King's highway;
We shoot the traps and rob the banks, and never run away.

Now the troopers they are all sent out to search the country round,
To bring in this notorious gang, but the Kellys can't be found.
The Kellys are in the ridges, the police drew up in ranks,
I think it's time, and off we go, and rob another bank.

I would never surrender to any coat of blue,
Or any man that wears a crown belong'ed to the crew.

They're game, there is no doubt of it, when they are on the beat,
But it took ten traps to take Ben Hall when he was fast asleep.

I'd rather die like Donahue, that bushranger so brave,
Than be taken by the government to be treated like a slave,
I'd rather fight with all my might as long as I'd eyes to see;
I'd rather die ten thousand deaths than die on the gallows tree.

Now all young men, take my advice, that's bent for a roving life;
Pray do not roam but stay at home, settle down and take a wife.
For if you go a-robbing upon the King's highway,
You'll have to fight with all your might, or else lay down and die.[3]

Oral traditional expressions of sympathy for the Kellys were not restricted to musicians and singers. The same sentiments infuse a very fine recitation, collected from the late Bill Shawcross of Lithgow by John Meredith during the 1950s. In 'Kelly Was Their Captain', Ned Kelly is celebrated in heroic terms — 'No better could be found'. Ned, Dan, and Mrs Kelly are said to be the objects of police and official persecution and the actions of the outlaws are justified as righteous revenge. The police are characterised as cowards and the bushrangers are said to have been finally betrayed by Aaron Sherritt. Historically this is incorrect; neither Sherritt or anyone else betrayed the Kellys at Glenrowan, though there is a widespread belief that he did. This folk poem provides a good example of the manner in which the Kelly legend has generated unhistorical details in accordance with the characteristics of the highwayman tradition—in this case the role of the traitor. Once again, what people believe is more important than the 'truth', at least it is in the world of folklore. The portrayal of Sherritt as the traitor in the Kelly story is one more indication of the way in which the facts become tailored to fit an existing traditional stereotype.

KELLY WAS THEIR CAPTAIN

Come all you wild colonial boys and attention to me pay,
For in my song I will unfold the truth without delay.
'Twas of a famous outlawed band that roamed this country round,
Ned Kelly was their captain and no finer could be found.

But the Governor of Victoria was an enemy of this man,
And a warrant he likewise put out to take his brother Dan.
But, alas, one day some troopers came young Dan to apprehend,
And he like a tiger stood at bay, his mother to defend.

Five hundred pounds reward was made for Ned, where'er was found,
And from place to place was hunted as if he was a hound.
Now driven to desperation to the bush brave Ned did take,
Young Dan, Steve Hart and brave Joe Byrne, all for his mother's sake.

And although they deemed them outlaws, brave men they proved to be,
And vengeance ranked [*sic*] in every breast for Kelly's misery.
They burnt his mother's vine-clad hut, which caused his heart to yearn,
And angered his companions, Dan, Steve, and brave Joe Byrne.

One day as Ned and his comrades in ambush were concealed,
They spied three mounted troopers and their presence did reveal.
They called to them 'Surrender', these words to them he said,
'Resist a man among you and I'll surely shoot you dead'.

It was at the Wombat Ranges where Ned Kelly made his haunt,
And all those Victorian troopers at that name would truly daunt.
For months they lay in ambush until finally were betrayed
By traitor Aaron Sherritt, and his life the treachery paid.

It was at the Glenrowan station where the conflict raged severe,
When more than fifty policemen at the scene then did appear.
No credit to their bravery, no credit to their name,
Ned Kelly terrified them all and put their blood to shame.[4]

A slightly different style of song is also a part of the oral tradition.
These are songs that usually have their origins in literary rather than
folk forms but, because of their essential sympathy with the outlaws, are
taken into the oral tradition and reworked to a greater or lesser extent
to fit the highwayman stereotype. These songs or poems are often recog-
nisable by the more flowery or literary style of lyrics and generally intro-

duce the figure of Kate Kelly as heroine. We shall have more to say about these pieces in relation to the media, but here is one song that seems to have started life in this way.

THE KELLY GANG

Come all young men with feel-ing with re - gret I must un- fold, I have a tale to tell of men whose hearts are stout and bold who now lie in their graves.

The odds against the Kelly gang
Were fifty if not more,
And yet there was not courage
For to face but only four.

Long life unto Kate Kelly,
For she was a noble girl;
She appeared upon the scene
In spite of all the world.

For true she loved her brothers,
Likewise the other two,
And so she proved to all the world.
Her heart was fair and true.

If any praise be due at all,
Then let the praise be gave
To those four unfortunates
Who now lie in their graves.[5]

While songs and poems like these were defending the Kellys or mourning their deaths another oral tradition associated with popular heroes was trying to bring at least one, often two, of the gang back to life. There was a persistent rumour that Dan Kelly and Steve Hart somehow survived the fire at Glenrowan. The two bushrangers were variously supposed to have made their getaway to America, South Africa, or, rather less exotically, to Goondiwindi. There was a strong popular belief that the two outlaws fought in the Boer War, sometimes with the Boers, sometimes against them, as in these letters, the first from a Melbourne *Herald* of 1930: 'It was reported when I was in South Africa during the Boer War that two of the gang were there, but I knew that couldn't be true. How the rumour originated I do not know, but I was asked about it more than once.'[6]

This particular belief was still about in 1967 when Ian Jones, Kelly scholar and filmmaker, received a letter containing this statement: 'My uncle a mining engineer was in South Africa during the Boer War. He met Dan Kelly and Steve Hart — they were fighting with the Boers.'[7]

And in 1933 the *Bulletin* commented upon the great number of men roaming around the country during the 1920s and early 1930s claiming to be Dan Kelly.[8] Somebody calling himself 'N.Q.' was even inspired to put pen to paper about the apparently universal survivor:

THE MYSTERY MAN

Going home in the dusk from the township
We passed an old man with his dog.
'Good evening' said we and 'Good evening', said he,
Then turned down a track by a log,
A quiet old track by a log.
And somebody said, 'Well, who'd think it?'
And 'What would you think then?' I said.
'Why, that man going home with his dog.
Going down on the track by the log,
He's no one but Kelly, *the* Kelly,
Dan Kelly, the brother of Ned!'

'But how can you know that?' I asked him.
He said, 'It's as plain as your nose.
From nowhere he came, with a vague sort of name,
And a beard that nobody grows,

No, nowadays nobody grows.
And kiddies won't pass him at twilight
And he talks to his dog, so it's said,
And it's all about watches and gold
And things that shouldn't be told,
So he's no one but Kelly, *the* Kelly,
Dan Kelly, the brother of Ned.'

Now that was in one little township,
But many such townships there be
From Mansfield to Sale or the Acheron Vale,
And one point in common you'll see,
They've all the one bogey to see.
For someone's said, 'Well, he's a caution!'
'That little old man there?' I've said.
'Yes, there's loot in his hut,
So he keeps the door shut,
For he's no one but Kelly, *the* Kelly
Dan Kelly, the brother of Ned.'

So bogeys will never be dead
While men get their dreams in their head,
And an old chap ready for bed
And tired with the life he's led,
Shearing in shed after shed
Or mining or farming instead,
Has got to be Kelly, *the* Kelly,
Dan Kelly, the brother of Ned![9]

The extent and persistence of this particular tradition is an expression of popular reluctance to accept the death of certain heroes. This is a universal phenomenon of folklore and includes figures as diverse as Arthur, 'the once and future king', Alexander I of Russia, and even Jesus of Nazareth.[10] Ned Kelly was undoubtedly the central hero of the Kelly saga, but he was just as surely executed in 1880. The popular need to believe in the survival of the hero was accordingly transferred to Dan and Steve whose bodies were charred beyond recognition in the final conflagration at Glenrowan. Perhaps this legend began in the whispering of the onlookers at Glenrowan station, many of whom later said they heard the sound of horses coming and going to the scene throughout the siege. However it began, the survival legend has been a continuous strand woven through the fabric of Kelly oral tradition and has been one of many points of interchange between it and the media tradition that evolved from the bushrangers' notoriety.

From the very beginning the Kellys' outlawry was a media event. After Stringybark Creek the urban and provincial newspapers had been almost continually agog with breathless reports and rumours about the gang. Within months of the murders postcards of the bushrangers were being sold throughout Victoria, a substantial pamphlet had been published in Mansfield and a broadsheet of Kelly songs had appeared in Hobart,

GLENROWAN ACCORDING TO THE NEWS MEDIA. (*AUSTRALASIAN SKETCHER*, 3 JULY 1880)

DESTRUCTION OF THE KELLY GANG. DRAWN BY MR. T. CARRINGTON DURING THE ENCOUNTER

THE AUSTRALASIAN SKETCHER

WEIGHT
97 pounds

NED KELLY'S ARMOUR. FROM A SKETCH MADE BY MR. T. CARRINGTON.
1—THE HELMET, FRONT VIEW. 2—SIDE VIEW OF HELMET. 3—BREASTPLATE. 4—BACK PLATE. 5—BACK CROTCH.
6—FRONT VIEW OF ARMOUR.

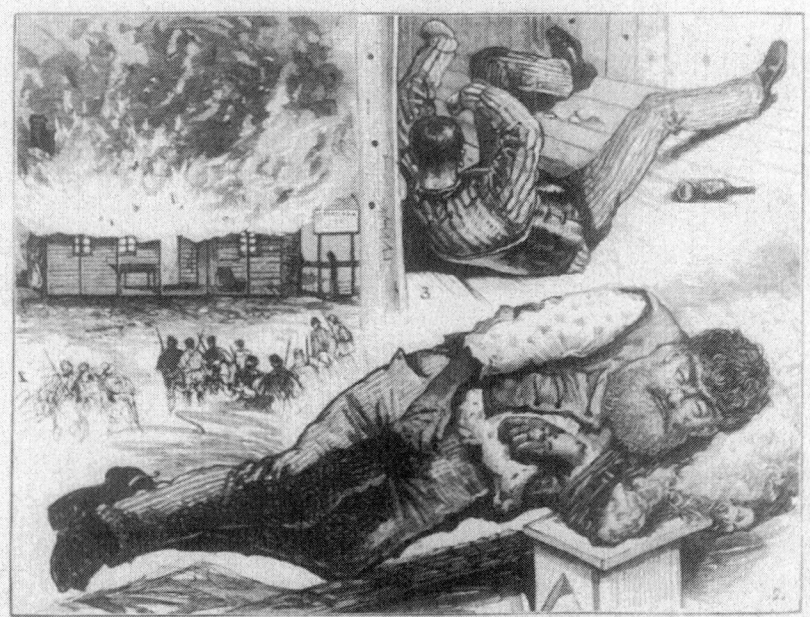

DESTRUCTION OF THE KELLY GANG. DRAWN BY MR. T. CARRINGTON DURING THE ENCOUNTER.
1—SETTING FIRE TO GLENROWAN HOTEL. 2—NED KELLY LYING ON BUNK IN STATION-MASTER'S HOUSE. 3—SCENE THROUGH
THE DOOR OF THE INN, BYRNE LYING DEAD ON THE FLOOR WHERE HE FELL JUST IN FRONT OF THE BAR.

Tasmania. While the gang was still at large a dramatic production that apparently portrayed the gang as heroes and the police as blundering oafs was, not surprisingly, suppressed by the authorities in Melbourne. All that remains of this play is the song 'We're the Jolliest Lot of Thieves', mentioned in chapter 1. Another song in very similar vein has recently been found in the papers of Charles Noble, a nineteenth-century concert singer who seems to have written this parody of a Schumann song in late 1879 or 1880 and to have performed it 'with success':

THE KELLYS' FOES

We are two courageous bobbies, just taken off our beat;
We are sent to catch the Kellys in their quiet snug retreat;
Oh if we come across them, and they think it is no harm—
We'll run them in, we'll run them in,
We'll run them in, we'll run them in,
We'll show them we're the bold gendarmes.

Of course we're very wary, and of ourselves we take good care.
To risk our precious lives we're chary; if danger looms, we won't be there;
But if we find them napping, for them we'll make it warm—
We'll run them in, etc.

Oh won't we have some boozing when eight thousand pounds we've got.
If we could catch them snoozing in some quiet sequestered spot;
Then we would quickly summon them, nor give the least alarm —
We'll run them in, etc.[11]

By 1880 an anonymous pamphlet called *History of the Outlaws* did not even need to specify its subject in the title. The same year saw the first issue of the *Bulletin* providing extensive coverage of the outlaws which it continued up to the time of Ned Kelly's execution. Succeeding years were filled with a constant stream of 'Kellyana' from a variety of sources, including the press, book publishers, magazines, poets and playwrights. 'The Little Digger', Billy Hughes, even made his contribution to the ever-growing Kelly chronicles with the tale of a bright weekend in Jerilderie.[12]

'THE LITTLE DIGGER' AT

JERILDERIE. (*HERALD*,

MELBOURNE, 10 JANUARY 1934)

MR HUGHES TELLS A TALE OF THE KELLY GANG

A Bright Week-end In Jerilderie

Specially written for The Herald
By Mr W. M. Hughes

MR W. M. HUGHES

NED KELLY

After contemplating the modern fashion in biographical writing, the veteran Parliamentarian turns to Australia's most famous outlaw band of the past, and, with many lively details, passes on a tale of its exploits.

IN recent years a number of writers of the first rank have turned their attention to biography, and have given the world books that will live; for quite apart from their style which bears the imprint of genius, they are storehouses of original research, revealing in many cases the great men of past ages in an entirely new light.

With some of these the contrast between the man as he is now portrayed and our concept of him as derived from conventional sources is really startling. When we read Mr Bryant's fascinating story of Charles II we realise how badly the Merry Monarch has been misunderstood and libelled. But what Mr Arthur Weigall has done for Nero and Cleopatra is perhaps even more remarkable. Pay he has shown us that Nero, far from being a monster, a tyrant, an incendiary sprang with a weakness for playing the fiddle, was a wise, humane and virtuous man and one of the greatest rulers of all time. As for Cleopatra, instead of being a

dark-eyed, voluptuous vamp, it now turns out that she was a beautiful blonde with a passion for philosophy and a distinct distaste for male society.

What has been done with such signal success for Nero and Cleopatra may be attempted with even less promising subjects. Someone may even rewrite the story of the Kellys so that generations of young Australians will see a rehabilitated Ned through the glamour of romance as the modest prototype of that other famous outlaw, Robin Hood. This classic I must leave to other and more gifted men, contenting myself here with this much less ambitious effort of telling in unpretentious prose the story of an incident in the career of that notorious and ill-fated man.

For this minor task I am not ill-equipped for only the other day I stumbled by good fortune on one who knew the Kellys intimately — who was, in fact, a blood relation of the family, a fine fellow, a magnificent horseman, and as honest as the sun; and heard from his lips the story of "How Ned Kelly robbed the Bank at Jerilderie."

Ned Kelly and his three followers, Dan Kelly, his brother, Steve Hart and Joe Byrne left their camp and struck out far from the Kelly homestead — which was about 11 miles out of Benalla — in the morning, and striking a direct line crossed the Murray near Yarrawonga and came into New South Wales.

The next day they made a bee line for Jerilderie and arrived at the outskirts of the town about three or four o'clock in the afternoon.

The day was Saturday and the populace was indulging in quiet relaxation after a week's strenuous toil. In the hotel, the Mecca of most of the male inhabitants, many pilgrims had already gathered when Ned, after a careful reconnaissance, arrived with his band. He promptly bailed up the hotel-keeper, his staff and the fabulous souls who were drinking at the bar. There was no trouble. The crowd, under the spell of the Kellys and their menacing guns, obeyed instructions as noiselessly as figures in a silent film.

Not the faintest ripple disturbed the placid life of Jerilderie. The landlord, by directions of Ned Kelly, remained in the bar, being deeply impressed with Ned's injunction that he was "to carry on business as usual." The drinkers were herded into the dining-room — a fine commodious apartment, which, as the day wore on, was to be uncomfortably crowded.

As each fresh customer came into the bar and after being duly served by the attentive landlord, he was ushered into the dining-room.

Ned Kelly Turns Reformer and Frees a Drunkard

ALL being quiet on the western front, Ned now proceeded to develop another stage in his plan of campaign. Leaving Dan in the bar and placing Steve Hart outside at the back, where he commanded a good view of the road and could see through the window into the dining-room, in which the patrons of the hotel were yarded, and giving Joe Byrne a roving commission to keep an eye lifting for unforeseen contingencies, Ned made his way leisurely down to the Police Station, which was on the outskirts of the town, half a mile or so from the hotel.

Arriving, he called out, "Is the police there?" At the sound of his voice Sergeant Devine came to the door, and, seeing Ned, asked what was the matter. To which Ned replied: "You ought to send some of your men down to the hotel, sergeant; they're murdering a man down there."

The sergeant looked at Ned in a puzzled way for a moment, sizing him up, and then said, "I can't send anybody, I'm all alone."

"In that case," said Ned in a business-like way, "stick 'em up! I'm Ned Kelly," pulling out his gun to give point to his command. The sergeant was a brave man, but he "stuck 'em up," and Ned came into the station and tied him up.

"Is there anyone in the lock-up?" asked Ned of the sergeant. "Yes," said the sergeant, "there's a drunk there; he's been there all day." "You'll have to let him out," said

Kelly. "I can't do that," protested the sergeant. "Now, I'm giving you a chance," said Ned. "You must let him out, for I've got to lock you in." The sergeant, accepting the inevitable, reluctantly agreed.

Ned took him to the lock-up, while he himself went in to the prisoner. Looking at the poor man and shaking his head reproachfully, Ned said, "This is a bad job for a man like you. The poor prisoner buried his head in his hands. "Look here," said Ned after a moment's silence, "I'm going to give you another chance. If you promise to clear out of the district at once I'll strain a point and let you out."

The poor "drunk"—by this time cold, sober and very sorry for himself, believing Ned be a policeman, probably an Inspector, fervently promised to clear out and leave it." He was duly released, and ... was placed in the cell and loc...

As Ned came away from ... ran plump up against M... man's wife who was loo... him his tea. "Give it to ... take it to him." Wh... Devine all of a ... replied Ned, Mrs ... much taken abo... so well with ... and calmed ...

"Don't ... or to ... the ...

until I've done what '
"But," said poor Mrs ... can't stay here, for '
for early Mass in th... about that," said ...
you a hand."

The poor wom... way. Her little ... husband, the ... Ned Kel... charge ... was n... the ... is ...

A Little ...

AT dusk the sergeant and M... way from th... house. M... '

In 1906 the new medium of cinematography made its first full-length Australian debut[13] with *The Story of the Kelly Gang*, initiating a series of at least five Australian feature films on the same subject, the most recent being the 1969 version starring rock singer Mick Jagger as a very celluloid Ned Kelly. An extract from a review of the 1934 production, *When The Kellys Rode*, gives a fair idea of the style and approach of most of these feature films:

> . . . the film is unedifying, unconvincing, and often laughable. It is surely time Australian producers forgot Ned Kelly and the man they could not hang. The objection of the police in New South Wales to the film is easy to understand. Although the gang steal horses, wound a policeman, kill three more, rob banks and kill Sherritt, they are presented sympathetically. The children in the audience cheer whenever the gang eludes the police. Fortunately, the film is so woefully acted that even children cannot take it very seriously . . . [14]

Even before the first Australian Kelly movie, the visual entertainment media were promoting the Kellys' image. In 1897 a sixteen-year-old boy named Joseph Watson fell in with a couple of 'showbiz' types who travelled around south-eastern Australia with a magic lantern show. (Magic lanterns were early versions of the modern slide projector with the pictures painted or engraved on glass slides which were manually drawn between the light source, either a tiny oil lamp or a candle, and the magic lantern lens, projecting the image on a wall or screen.) Seventy-six years later Joe Watson remembered a typical magic lantern show:

COVER OF PROGRAMME FOR THE FILM *THE STORY OF THE KELLY GANG*, 1906. (NATIONAL FILM ARCHIVES, CANBERRA)

> . . . We'd arrive at the station on the weekend and line up a program for Sunday night. Paddy

POSTER FOR *THE STORY OF*
THE KELLY GANG. (NATIONAL
FILM ARCHIVES, CANBERRA)

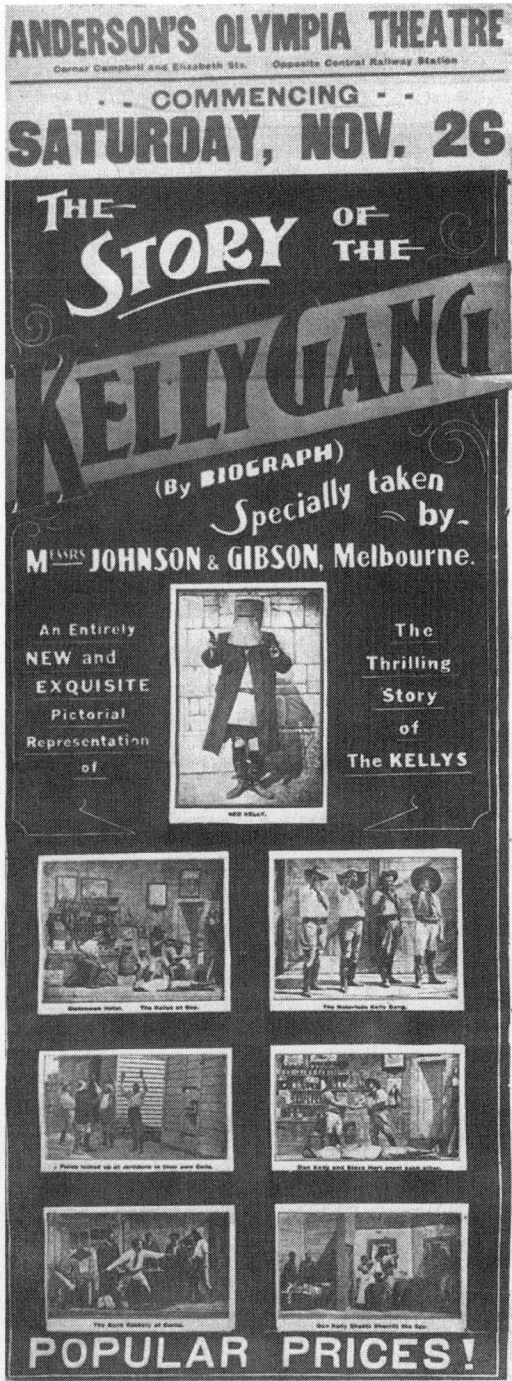

[owner of the show] would make a big show of the arrival, lots of noise and banners. We'd charge the public 2/6d each for a night of magic lantern slides songs and mechanical films with barrel-organ accompaniment . . . We had pictures of animals in the London Zoo, Countries of Europe, the Royal Family and the popular scandals of the day – 'The Dick Marr Case', 'The Paddy Creek Case', 'The Dean Case', 'The Butler Case of Sydney and the Goldfields', and of course we had a series on the Kelly Gang. The murders and bloodthirsty subjects were always the most popular – even with the womenfolk.[15]

When the Kelly gang slides were shown it was Joe Watson's job to sing 'The Ballad of the Kelly Gang' as a form of commentary for the story that was being projected on the wall in front of an obviously delighted audience. Mr Watson still remembered all sixteen verses of the song and they are a close variant of the 1879 version given in chapter 1. Regrettably the Kelly gang lantern slides have disappeared but their existence and Mr Watson's testimony to their popularity are further indications of the early media utilisation of the Kelly story and the long-standing receptivity of the general public.

BELOW: NED KELLY SHOOTS
CONSTABLE FITZPATRICK IN
THE STORY OF THE KELLY GANG.
(NATIONAL FILM ARCHIVES, CANBERRA)

BOTTOM: THE CAPTURE OF NED
KELLY IN *THE STORY OF THE KELLY
GANG.* (NATIONAL FILM ARCHIVES, CANBERRA)

CAPTURE OF NED KELLY

GLENROWAN TRACK IN THE FILM *NED*

KELLY, 1970, AND

MICK JAGGER AS NED KELLY, 1970. (NATIONAL

FILM ARCHIVES, CANBERRA)

During the 1930s an infant local broadcasting and recording industry finally found its Australian voice in the form of country music, originally copied from American recordings. Country music in the United States had its own tradition of 'badman' heroes and after the initial wave of mindless imitation had subsided a little, Australian singers began looking for local heroes to balladise. In a country still reeling from the effects of the Depression they did not have to look far to find an Australian champion of the poor and dispossessed. In 1939 Tex Morton and 'Smiling' Billy Blinkhorn (an immigrant from Canada) both recorded songs about Ned Kelly on 78-r.p.m. records for Regal Zonophone. These were to be followed by numerous Australian country songs celebrating the Kellys and sung by such popular and big-selling artists as Slim Dusty, Smoky Dawson, and Buddy Williams.[16]

The basic ingredients of these media treatments of the Kelly story were derived from existing oral traditions. Probably the most widely used aspect was the concept of the outlaws, particularly Ned, as brave resourceful men who 'died game'. Even the earliest pot-boilers, while deploring the violence of Stringybark Creek, generally admire the gang's daring, bushmanship and sheer style. Twelve years after the outbreak even *The Banker's Magazine* felt able to admit that Ned Kelly was 'a thorough bushman and a born general . . . He was a powerful, handsome man and an all-round athlete; he never interfered with women', and that he went to his death 'very quietly and coolly'.[17]

Thirty-odd years later the same mixed feelings were still evident. A romance titled *The Girl Who Helped Ned Kelly* 'created a greater sensation than any other Australian romance' when it appeared serially in *Table Talk* during 1928. The foreword to the 1929 publication in book form of this work had this to say about Ned: 'Superb qualities of leadership, almost unexampled endurance and uncanny bushcraft, would have taken him far if Fate had willed for him a more honest career.'[18]

Examples like these could be cited almost endlessly from the never-ending flood of Kelly literature. The same ambivalence was also a feature of the Kelly films. A silent production of 1923, *The True Story of the Kelly Gang*, wobbled its confused way to a moralising conclusion through portrayals of Constable Fitzpatrick as a hard-line trooper, the police firing first at Stringybark Creek, and the Kellys' 'countless sympathisers', who, we are later informed, only did it for the money. Just before the end Ned 'says' of his impending death:

THE END OF THE 1923 FILM *THE TRUE STORY OF THE KELLY GANG*. (NATIONAL FILM ARCHIVES. CANBERRA)

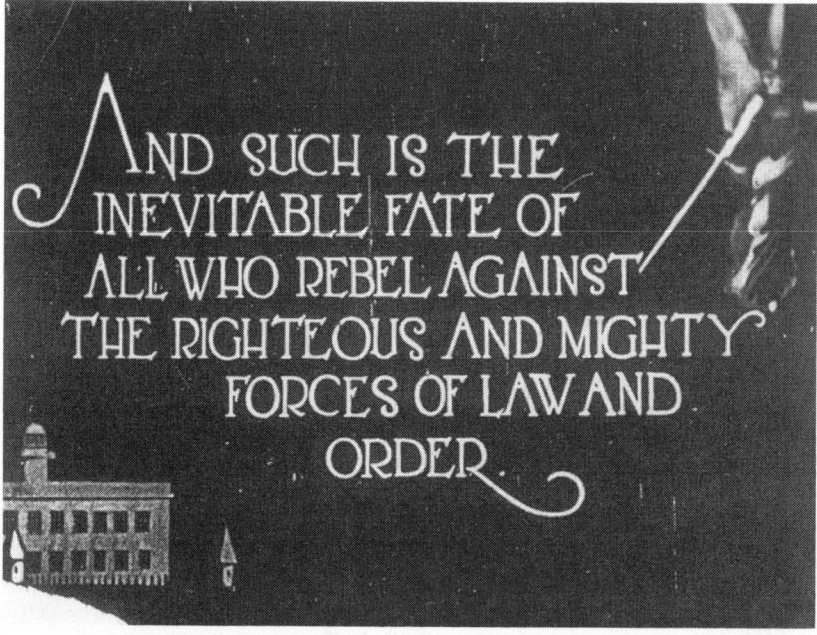

AND SUCH IS THE INEVITABLE FATE OF ALL WHO REBEL AGAINST THE RIGHTEOUS AND MIGHTY FORCES OF LAW AND ORDER.

The film then cuts to a final card:

THE WAGES OF SIN IS DEATH

as Ned bravely faces the noose.

Media productions also used the highwayman concept of the outlaw as the victim of circumstances largely beyond his control. In the oral tradition this takes the form of unjust police persecution. The media were often concerned to white-wash the activities of the police as much as possible, so the same basic idea was expressed in a number of ways. Number 44 of the Boy's Friend 3d. Library, for instance, was titled *Ned Kelly: A Tale of Trooper and Bushranger* and written as an Australian 'western' complete with faithful steeds, ranches, and an Aboriginal who talked like a Hollywood Red Indian — 'Me see um track,' and so on. In this undated paperback Ned is said to have 'gone wrong' because of a woman and does not seem able to make up his mind whether he should be wearing the black hat or the white.[19] There have been many similar Deadwood Dick fabrications over the last hundred years.[20]

A wildly inaccurate film made in 1951, *The Glenrowan Affair*, shows the police as bullying heavies and says that Mrs Kelly is in Melbourne gaol merely for 'being Ned Kelly's mother'. The latest film, *Ned Kelly*, also takes the view that economic circumstances and persecution were the main causes of Ned's outlawry as, indeed, do the two country songs from the 1930s which both suggest that Ned never really had a chance. Tex Morton's effort begins with this verse:

Ned Kelly was born in a ramshackle hut,
He'd battled since he was a kid,
He grew up with bad men and duffers and thieves
And learned all the bad things they did.

Billy Blinkhorn's 'Poor Ned Kelly' says, a little inanely, though the meaning is plain:

The coppers used to bully his poor old mum,
So he stole their horses just for fun.

Both these songs have taken on a life beyond the confines of the discs that carried them and have been adapted into the continuing Kelly oral tradition.[21] It is not hard to understand why. Apart from the few lines already mentioned, both songs contain the implication that Ned's actions, real or imagined, were a kind of counter-stroke on behalf of the deprived against the system that made them poor, or against the wealthy who kept them that way, a potent idea to the battlers of the Depression. Billy Blinkhorn sings:

Poor Ned Kelly, it's easier to do today
Poor Ned Kelly, you don't even have to run away,

and finishes with the verse:

(spoken) But what with income tax and
sales tax and other taxes, the price of
taxi cabs and the way they charge these days
for a few beers and a packet of smokes, I say
to myself, 'Old Ned and his mates they weren't
such bad blokes'.

Tex Morton's song has a very similar conclusion:

When I look round at some people I know,
And the prices of things that we buy;
I just think to myself, well, perhaps after all,
Old Ned wasn't such a bad guy.

And if Ned was not exactly robbing the rich to give to the poor in a very early popularisation, *Ned Kelly, the Ironclad Australian Bushranger*, published in thirty-eight weekly instalments during 1881 by

'HE HEROINE WARNS THE BUSHRANGER
F APPROACHING DANGER' FROM AN 1881
ERIALISATION.

ONE OF NED KELLY'S MORE BIZARRE
EXPLOITS IN THE SERIALISATION.

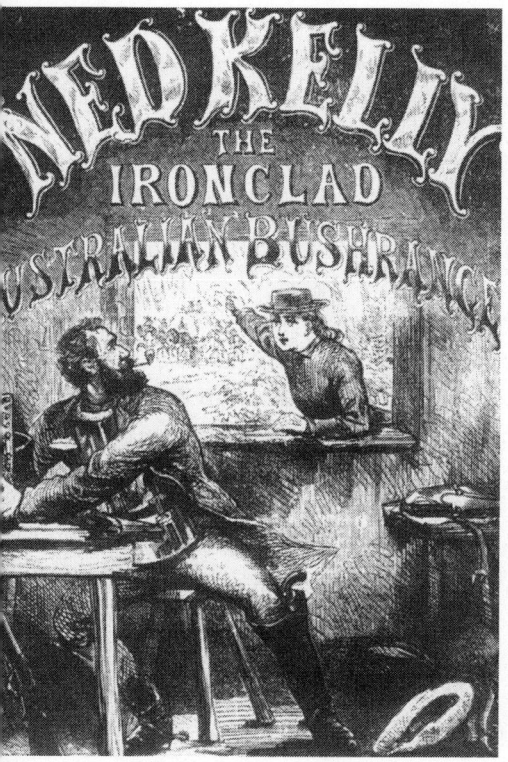

a quick-witted English publisher, at least his heart was in the right place. Between fictional travels around the world to undertake a stunning variety of criminal activities, Ned finds time to tell his equally fictional adopted daughter: 'It's no sin, in my case, to rob a rascally government who robbed my father and mother of life.'[22]

More recently, Douglas Stewart's play, *Ned Kelly*, gathers into itself many of the Kelly traditions. Broadcast as a radio drama in 1942 and published the following year, the play treats Ned as a direct successor to Ben Hall and the notion of the gallant highwayman: 'Bow to the ladies! Kiss the blooming babies', a disgruntled Steve Hart says to Ned in Act 2, Scene 2 when the outlaw leader makes him return the watch stolen from Reverend Gribble. Stewart sees Kelly as an ambivalent Australian archetype and, significantly, ends the play with the capture of the defiant armoured outlaw rather than with his execution.

The legend of Dan Kelly's survival after the Glenrowan fire also spawned its share of media exploitation. In 1911 the prolific sensationalist, Ambrose Pratt, foisted a cleverly conceived book upon the Australian public. It was comprehensively titled, *Dan Kelly, Being the Memoirs of Daniel Kelly (Brother of Edward Kelly, Leader of the Kelly Gang of Bushrangers), Supposed to Have Been Slain in the Famous Fight at Glenrowan.* In fact, the book was one of Pratt's concoctions, though this did not prevent it from running into numerous reprints over the next few years.

J. J. Kenneally, the partisan author of *The Complete Inner History of the Kelly Gang and Their Pursuers* (1929), was particularly incensed at this and similar fakes, as were the members of the Kelly family still living at Greta, old Mrs Kelly and Jim, the other brother. Kenneally even managed to get Jim Kelly to write or endorse a review of his book that included a spirited denunciation of the impostors. As this extract from the review shows, the family kept up with the Kelly literature and, understandably, were not very happy with what they read:

> The name of my brother Dan has been used freely for sordid gain by a gang of impostors, as well as by the underworld of the journalistic profession. Some correspondence appeared recently in a Melbourne paper, in which it was claimed that my brother Dan had escaped from the siege of Glenrowan. This fabrication is set at rest by the sworn testimony, given verbatim in your book, by the Very Rev. Dean Gibney (afterwards Bishop of Perth, W.A.), who is rightly described as 'The Hero of Glenrowan.'
>
> . . . I myself have been impersonated by depraved impostors. A bookseller (canvasser) in Sydney passed himself off as 'Jim Kelly', brother of Ned Kelly. He was a short, stout man, whereas I am over 6 feet in height. He told a tale that he was not allowed to live in Greta, whereas I have not been away from Greta for over 50 years.
>
> A statement appeared recently in a Melbourne paper that a fellow named Brown claimed to be my brother, Dan Kelly. Now, there are certain marks on the body of my brother Dan by which I can identify him if he were still alive, but any impostor will give me a wide berth, because I can destroy the impostor's field of exploitation so favoured by the lowest stratum of the 'white' race.
>
> For filthy lucre mercenary writers have, from time to time, indulged

in outrageous libels against the Kellys. These unfortunates still cling to the belief that judicial bias is as strong as ever, and that I have no chance of getting a fair deal in a claim for libel in the 'law courts.' Your book has so encouraged me that I intend to deal drastically, in the future, with every libeller of my family.

'The Girl Who Helped Ned Kelly.' This book is another example of mercenary journalism. My brother was so devoted to his mother that he had no 'girl'. Of course, the author of the book above referred to protected himself by calling his concoction 'a novel.' A more recent concoction is being published in a daily paper for the purpose of increasing or maintaining its circulation.

As an effective exterminator of the hive of journalistic wasps, your book would have been a great consolation to my dear mother if it had been published before her death. I regret that my mother is not alive to see her family so completely vindicated by your book.

Wishing that your book will be found in every home in Australia.

I am,

Yours sincerely,

(Signed) James Kelly[23]

Jim Kelly died in 1945, aged eighty-six. If he had lived a few years longer he might have been as irritated by the film *The Glenrowan Affair* as he had been by earlier exploitations of Dan's alleged survival. The film used the device of an old man telling the Kelly story. At the end it was revealed that the old man's excellent knowledge of events was due to his being the real Dan Kelly, having lived incognito in the Kelly country since 1880. Once again, a facet of the oral tradition provided the basis for a media production.

These elements, Ned Kelly's bravery, his forced or, at least unintentional, outlawry, his championing of the poor and the survival legends were digested and regurgitated by the media in one form or another to cater for a voracious Kellyana appetite. But the media also contributed some new ingredients to the mix. One of these was a fascination with the armour worn by the outlaws at Glenrowan. This occurs without fail in books, films, poems, plays, even Nolan's paintings, but is not found in oral tradition — with the minor exception of a line in Billy Blinkhorn's 'Poor Ned Kelly' which mentions the armour in passing.

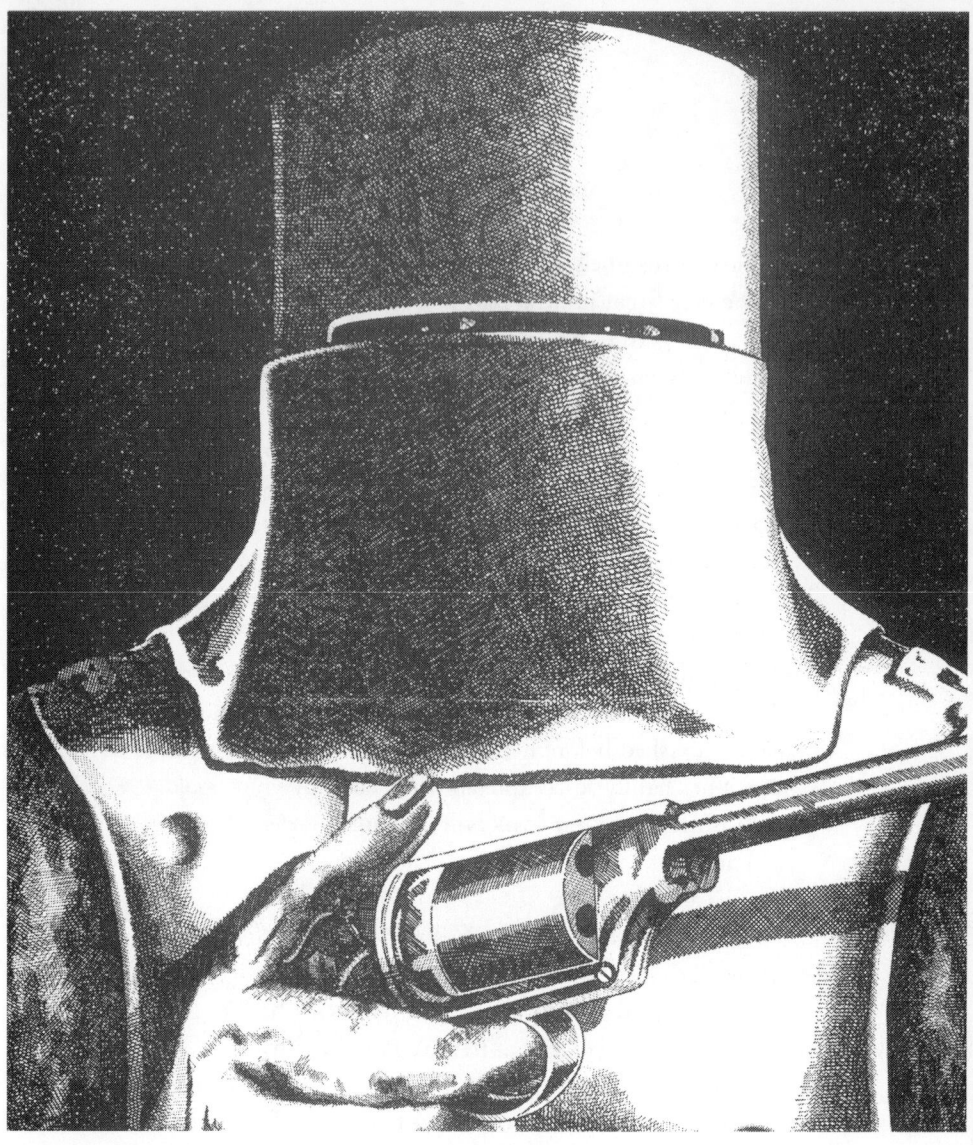

Perhaps this is the thin end of the wedge and orally transmitted Kelly songs collected a century from now will all mention the outlaw's armour.

A COLONIAL MUTUAL ADVERTISEMENT. (*THE SUN*, SYDNEY, 22 JULY 1980)

Another prominent feature of the media rarely found in oral tradition is the tendency to moralise about the Kellys. We have already seen this at its most blatant in the film, *The True Story of Ned Kelly*, and it may be found in the last verse of 'Ye Sons of Australia', a long and dreary poem by J. K. Moir, first published in the *Bulletin*. But in a version of this poem, collected as a song from oral tradition during the 1950s, the moralistic conclusion and details of the armour have been dropped. The lyrics have been considerably pruned and amended to create a totally different meaning from the original:

YE SONS OF AUSTRALIA

Ye sons of Aust-ra-lia, for-get not the brave and gath-er wild flo-wers to place on their graves. They were four dar-ing out-laws, their race it is run – And we'll lay on their tomb-stones the lau-rels they've won.

To the banks of Euroa they made their first dash,
They cleared out its gold and they steered for the bush.
Blacktrackers and troopers on guard were at hand,
But they wiped out their enemies where'er they drew hand.

Now this gallant Kate Kelly was noble of mien,
She would sit on her horse like some new-born queen,
She would ride through the forest, revolver in hand,
Regardless of danger and errant of hand.

May the great god of angels protect as of old,
May her name be regarded in letters of gold.
Her brothers were outlaws, she loved them most dear,
And she hastened to tell them when danger was near.[24]

The idea of drawing a moral from the Kelly tale is alien to the oral tradition. But as 'Ye Sons of Australia' illustrates, one media innovation that did find a degree of acceptance in oral tradition is the notion of Kate Kelly as heroine. This is a commonplace of all the Kelly media material and is found in those traditional songs that are recognisably derived from literary, nineteenth-century sources, such as 'Farewell to Greta' and 'The Kelly Gang'. Just why this aspect of the Kellys' media image has been received into oral tradition while the armour motif has met with scant acceptance and the moralising tendency with none at all is a matter for speculation. There are plenty of precedents for female figures in general folk tradition, but none at all for armoured bush-rangers and very little for moral conclusions. Therefore, Kate has become a part of both the media and oral Kelly traditions while the armour and the moralising have remained fairly firmly with the media. At least, that is how things stand at the moment. We are obviously dealing with an ongoing, living complex of traditions that are capable of many adaptations. While they still retain any social significance they will continue to evolve in response to the needs which they satisfy.

Whatever the reasons for the variable appeal of these elements, the media have continued to offer an overwhelming variety of material to the apparently insatiable public fascination with Ned Kelly. Barely a year has passed in the last hundred without the publication of one or, more often, a number of works aimed at this seemingly eternal audience. To a greater or lesser extent they all display the same ambiguities and bewilderment about Ned Kelly. Was he a hero or a villain? One of the most frequently reprinted Kelly pot-boilers, the Reverend W. H. Fitchett's *Ned Kelly and His Gang*, provides an example of this confusion. Before proceeding on a severe anti-Kelly, pro-police rendition of events, the author says: 'And yet, the four scoundrels who formed the Kelly gang will be remembered — in certain districts at least — with an unashamed admiration when all other criminals are forgotten.' [25]

An even more explicit illustration of Australian attitudes towards Ned Kelly is contained in a work published by its author, Henry H. Neary, in Sydney, probably sometime during the 1930s. In this book, barely more than a pamphlet, Neary succinctly and accurately delineates the essence of Ned Kelly's popular image:

> The Kellys became a sort of tradition in Australia, much as Dick Turpin did in England and the James brothers in U.S.A. [sic] Until 1915 their memory was regarded in a somewhat heroic light, but after the advent of the Anzacs and their deeds on Gallipoli and the deeds of the Light Horse in Egypt and Palestine, this country found itself with a new and much worthier tradition — the tradition of Anzac, with its spirit of mateship, sacrifice and courage. All the same, it was the same daring blood that inspired the bushmen of the first A.I.F. that had enabled the Kelly gang to defy the police for so long and gave them the courage to fight to the death when cornered. Wrong as

they were, and black as was their criminal record, they had two great attributes in their bushman-ship and bravery, and it was probably that which led so many people to see only their courage rather than their criminality in the years that followed their violent end.[26]

Mr Neary was wrong about Ned's heroism being superseded by the Anzac tradition. As the verses in chapter 9, titled 'Ned Kelly Was a Gentleman', show, Ned Kelly's qualities were felt to be just as appropriate for fighting the Japanese as for fighting the Hun two and a half decades earlier.

Uncertainty about Ned's proper position on the spectrum between righteousness and damnation is also found in Australian folk speech.

Because they are largely subconscious, formalised expressions are an interesting indication of the conflicts and tensions generated by the co-existence of the oral and media Kelly traditions. Sayings like 'Game as Ned Kelly' or 'Game as the Kelly Gang' reflect admiration for the pluck and daring of the bushrangers. On the other hand, to accuse someone of using 'Kelly methods' or hinting at unfair tactics with the statement, 'They hanged Ned Kelly', is to recognise the criminal aspects of the bushranger.[27] The presence of these contrasting expressions in the Australian vernacular provides a nice illustration of the ambiguous attitudes towards Ned Kelly that thrive quite happily side-by-side in our society and in the minds of many people. There is even a Kelly joke that derives its rather laboured humour from the name of the property near Euroa where the bushrangers made their base during the robbery of the bank: 'Why are the Kelly Gang good matchmakers?' 'Because they took young women to young husbands', is the punchline![28]

That is perhaps a good note upon which to finish this examination of two traditions that have coalesced to form Ned Kelly's image in Australian popular tradition. The main thrust of the oral tradition has been to project Ned as an outlaw hero of the first magnitude. We know that this is an extension of a very widespread highwayman tradition which the media used as a basic sales-pitch. However, to avoid the censure of the respectable elements of society the Kellys' criminal aspects had to be stressed along with their more marketable attributes. And, of course, the police force could not be criticised too harshly. In fact, cleaning up the role of the police probably attracted a wider audience. This attitude naturally led to a moralising tendency, and the media evocation of the bushranger was completed with the addition of a heroine in the form of Kate Kelly or some *femme fatale* who either helps or undoes Ned. These two traditions have developed concurrently and merged in the popular mind to create an enduring image of an archetypal Australian hero.

CHAPTER
9
THE CONTINUING IMAGE OF NED KELLY

W e have seen how Ned Kelly's popular image evolved through the growth and interaction of oral and media versions of his story. As well as these songs, books and films Ned Kelly's persistent appeal is exploited in a number of other ways, including television, tourism and art, and even politics.

The media continued to show a strong interest in Ned and his activities, real or imagined. The centenary year of his death saw numerous Kelly articles and related snippets in metropolitan, regional, and national newspapers and periodicals. The Victorian Film Corporation had a Kelly documentary in the pipeline and Kelly student Ian Jones was producing a multimillion-dollar television series titled 'The Last Outlaw' for presentation on screens around the country. The manufacturers of a famous make of cameras and films purveyed their wares on television using an actor dressed in Kelly armour who insisted on only their brand of film: 'I wouldn't shoot anything else', claimed this TV bandit with the quick camera-finger.

A more localised commercial application of the bushranger's familiarity was to be found in Sydney. A firm of real-estate agents named Kelly and Sons specialised in selling homes around the inner suburbs. For their advertising copy the firm adopted a representation of the bush-

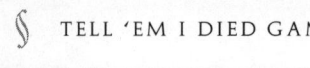

NED KELLY CENTENARY YEAR 1880-1980
A PARDON FOR NED!
Kelly Centenary Committee, P.O. Box J73 Brickfield Hill 2000.

ranger's metal headgear accompanied by the slogan, 'You're in Kelly Country'.

Down in the Kelly country proper, the tourist industry celebrated the outlaw for all he was worth. The Glenrowan Tourist Centre specialised in a bewildering array of Kellyana, from reproductions of the old postcards and reward posters to what were then recent editions of J. J. Kenneally's book. Wearing your Ned Kelly T-shirt and mask, clutching a replica of Ned's Colt pistol, you could wander through a display of fibreglass figures of police and bushrangers forever fighting a mute, static parody of the last stand. There were Kelly gang tea towels, badges, mugs, bells . . . even sticks of Ned Kelly rock, an imported English confectionery with 'Ned Kelly' impregnated all the way through. Business was brisk.

In Euroa and Mansfield the centennial celebrations passed off 'in one way or another' as a Sydney newspaper phrased it at the time. And, not to be outdone by the Victorians, the New South Wales town of Jerilderie staged a two-week extravaganza of general carousing and historical re-enactments of the gang's appearance a century before. The council even had Ned's armoured headpiece incorporated into the town's coat-of-arms.

The centenary year of Ned Kelly's death also generated an organisation calling itself the Ned Kelly Centenary Committee. As well as printing car bumper-stickers, organising festivals, and conducting various social activities, the committee wanted Ned Kelly to have a posthumous pardon.

On a slightly more serious note is the manner in which Ned Kelly has continued to be regarded by certain sections of the left in Australia. Some groups of this persuasion tend to see traditional art forms, particularly folksongs, as expressions of the collective soul of 'The People', untainted by crass bourgeois culture. As the previous chapter should have shown, this view is, to say the least, unrealistic. Folk tradition is in a process of continual interaction with literary cultural forms. Nevertheless, the idea of 'the folk' as an homogeneous, exploited entity with the consequent potential for political activation is an attractive and persistent notion. Ned is seen as a revolutionary leader of the oppressed against the capitalist exploiters. This attitude is inherent in John Manifold's poem 'The Death of Ned Kelly' and in a more recent song titled

KELLY'S SKULL STOLEN

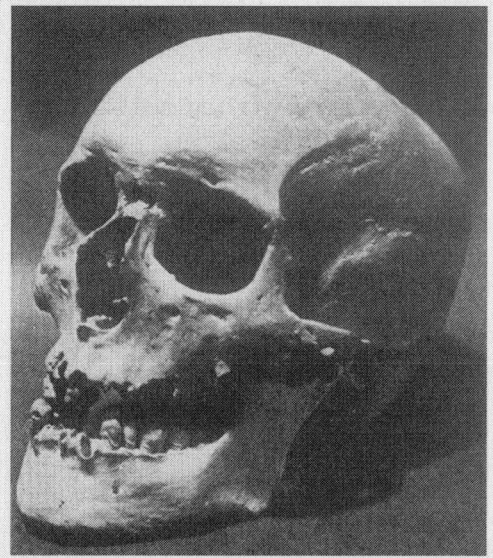

MELBOURNE. — Ned Kelly's skull was stolen yesterday from the old Melbourne jail in Russell Street — the place where he was hanged 98 years ago.

Police said the curator noticed that the skull was missing about 4 pm. It was in a glass case with other skulls and death masks. The case had not been smashed.

The chairman of the National Trust Mr Rodney Davidson, said it appeared that nothing else had been disturbed.

"It is a senseless act," he said. "The skull can't be of any monetary value to anyone but it is irreplaceable."

"I just hope whoever has the skull will look after it and see fit to return it."

The skull had been on display since the jail was opened to the public in 1972.

REPORT OF NED KELLY'S SKULL BEING STOLEN.

(SYDNEY MORNING HERALD, 3 DECEMBER 1978)

'Poor Ned' which uses the final verse of Manifold's poem.[1] Interestingly, although both pieces were written in conscious imitation of folksong style, neither appears to have found a place in oral tradition.

Perhaps stimulated by all the fuss, someone in 1978 stole what was alleged to be Ned's skull from its exhibition-case in the Melbourne Police Museum where it had rested for some years without exciting any unusual interest. Did the skull go to lie forgotten in some corner of a university college, the spoil of an impetuous student prank, or to grace the illicit collection of an unscrupulous Australiana buff? Whatever the answer, its disappearance was some sort of further testimony to the compelling magnetism that all things Kelly continue to exert.

Sidney Nolan's various series of Kelly paintings and tapestries, begun in 1946, hint at the theme of Ned Kelly as Christ crucified. Nolan's obsessive vision of the bushranger contrasts sharply with Manning Clark's depiction of Ned as a satanic thug in his 1968 contribution to the Wangaratta Seminar.[2] Nolan's and Clark's views are the opposite poles of the Kelly myth. Somewhere in between are the more mundane though perhaps more telling trivialities. For example, the Victorian government's official attitude to the Kelly Centenary was to ignore it. Not surprisingly, the Victoria Police Force was reluctant to have one of its less than glorious episodes dragged through the historical mire. In Mansfield, a centennial memorial service was held on 26 October 1978. Three riderless police horses, draped in black and with their stirrups reversed, were led to a ceremony that included no reference to the Kellys at all. Indeed, the Mansfield monument to the three troopers who died at Stringybark Creek, erected in 1880, bears this inscription:

> . . . in memory of the three brave men who lost their lives while endeavouring to capture a band of armed criminals in the Wombat Ranges . . .

The town of Mansfield and the Victoria Police would have preferred the Kellys to have remained anonymous criminals. But they were fighting a legend. The police only captured a man at Glenrowan and a convicted murderer was hanged a few months later. Ned Kelly goes on and on, even in officialdom. The federal government, having no skeletons to fear, issued a commemorative envelope for the battle at Glenrowan, despite the objections of the Queensland Police Union who agreed with the Victoria Police Association's contention that Ned Kelly should not be glorified in this manner. A Queensland spokesman for Australia Post disagreed: 'People look on Kelly as a folklore hero and not as the criminal that he was', the spokesman was reported to have said.

The Siege of Glenrowan ~ Centenary 1980

From this brief sampling of the offerings current at the time, it is clear that the figure of the bushranger has a multitude of applications and can manifest itself in many forms and contexts other than those that make up the bulk of this book. Although the sheer variety of Kellyana is another indication of Ned Kelly's wide popular appeal, most of the things mentioned in this chapter are the effects rather than the causes of the phenomenon. The fundamental reasons for Ned Kelly's development from bushranger to national hero over the century or more since his execution can be found in the occurrence of a number of social and historical coincidences.

Ned Kelly's initial impetus towards superstardom resulted from the existence of an Australian variant of an oral tradition reaching back at least to the legend of Robin Hood. This highwayman tradition flourished here, and informed the activities and status of local bandit heroes like Jack Donahue, Frank Gardiner, and Ben Hall. Kelly was the final flowering of these extensive and powerful roots of rural protest and direct action. He rapidly became a folk hero, a local bandit who adheres to the moral code of his social equals and acts as a violent and vicarious avenger for the years of dirty dealing that his supporters feel they have suffered at the hands of the rich and powerful. In the case of northeastern Victoria during the 1860s and 1870s the oppressive forces were believed to be squatters and the police in particular and the 'Crown' or government in general. The selectors of the area, from whose ranks the Kelly gang arose, saw themselves, not without justification, as the poor and oppressed. They saw Ned Kelly, if not as their salvation, then at least as their consolation.

While these local tensions were working themselves out the spectacular nature of the Kellys' precipitation into outlawry made instant headlines for newspapers around the country. The electric telegraph sparked the luridly embroidered details of Stringybark Creek across the world and continued to keep the press almost instantaneously informed of the daring and very readable exploits of the bushrangers. It was an age that craved for romance and the Kellys seemed to be the very essence of a rapidly receding romantic past. As we have seen, this was a characteristic that the media were not slow to exploit.

Glenrowan, of course, really gave the press an ultimate scoop and the media a continuing basis for the production of Kellyana. In its essential dynamics the burnt and bloody end of the outbreak was a dramatic performance.[3] All the major protagonists were present on the stage; the bushrangers and the police both had an eye for theatrical effect, it seems: the Kellys with their surreal armour and the police in their delayed entrance by train at dead of night. Throughout the siege there was an audience of up to five hundred people watching the show, alternately cheering and jeering the actors as they made their entrances and exits as if in accordance with some unseen but compelling script. After a day-long run, the climax came in the early morning mist when an armoured Ned Kelly, the main protagonist, thundered back onto the stage from the wings, gun blazing, and single-handedly engaged the assembled forces of the enemy. Finally, this 'apparition' was brought crashing to the ground by an underhand shotgun blast from Sergeant Steele, whose 'spiritual home was the scullery of Buckingham Palace', according to Max Brown.[4]

It was magnificent stuff; the anti-climax lingered on in an atmosphere of despair, finally erupting in an apocalypse of fire, charred bodies, and women weeping.

But the final curtain had not yet been rung down. A wider audience was to be given an unexpected bonus performance. The outlaw leader was not dead of his many wounds after all. He stood a trial that ended in a prophetic dialogue with his condemner, gained an unexpected surge of public support and agitation for his reprieve, and finally went to the gallows calmly and bravely like all good heroes of romance and folklore. Once again there was an audience — two in fact: a large one outside the prison and a smaller official one to witness the real end of the tragedy on the scaffold's final stage.

Not surprisingly, the media wanted the show to go on forever; so did the audience. With supply and demand so closely matched the entrepreneurs utilised those aspects of the drama that they knew were popular. Most of these elements were derived from the Kelly oral traditions. The media adoption and adaptation of these elements, together with one or two additions of their own, transmuted Ned Kelly's image into that of the romantic bandit hero who was a friend to the poor, fought and died bravely for his beliefs, and was not without some justice in his struggle.

But that was not quite enough. Bandit heroes were in plentiful supply, from Robin Hood to Jesse James to Ben Hall. Another element was needed to transform Ned Kelly's image into something essentially Australian. This was provided by the concurrent development of a rural myth, first delineated by Russel Ward in his book *The Australian Legend*.

The Kelly saga took place during a crucial period in Australia's development. The 1880s were perhaps the last years in which Australia could be said to have had a pioneering frontier. With the possible exception of the far north and parts of the interior, the great exploration was over. Most of the significant discoveries had been made and the urban centres were firmly established as the sources of political and economic influence. For many people the excitement of a pioneering life had passed or existed only in romantic recreations of an era that had ended. Most Australians lived in the cities and the classic figure of the bushman was increasingly pushed back to the remote, unpeopled interior of the country and into myth. The image of Ned Kelly as it existed in oral tradition contained many of the defining traits of that myth. He was strong, brave, resourceful, independent, a fine bushman, a male loner, loyal to his mates and implacably opposed to just about all forms of authority.

The bush ethos and the near-legendary characters who allegedly populated it were promoted through the *Bulletin*, the works of Paterson, Lawson, and their imitators, and through the general Australian folk tradition which is strongly bush-oriented. It received a boost during Australia's participation in the Boer War but developed into something like a religious creed only after Gallipoli. The romantic vision of a rural Australian superman was confirmed in the eyes of most by the mistaken belief that the 1st AIF was composed almost exclusively of boys from the bush, and that the remainder were urban larrikins who, despite their lurid pasts, possessed some of the ideal virtues of the bushman and had done the right thing in the hour of their country's need. Ned Kelly, with his outstanding qualifications, was ideally suited for a place in this pantheon and the slightly awkward fact that he had murdered three policemen faded to insignificance amidst the impersonal butchery of 'the war to end all wars'.

During the depression of the 1930s another aspect of Ned's existing image was reinforced. The widespread hardship and loss suffered by many people during this period fostered a tendency to see the bushranger as a friend of the poor and the dispossessed. It is significant that the main medium through which this view was both reflected and projected was Australian country music, with its idealised celebration of rural life and emphasis on the heroic bushman figure. We have already seen how some of these songs were taken into oral tradition, a sure sign that they had struck a responsive chord.

The image of the bushranger hero was invoked once again in World War II. An anonymous song from the period, titled 'Ned Kelly Was a Gentleman', portrays Ned as an Australian culture hero, a potential saviour whose 'mettle' might have preserved the country from an impending 'yellow flood', the perennial Australian nightmare. Even in so recent a song as this the highwayman element is firmly proclaimed as one of Ned's numerous virtues.

NED KELLY WAS A GENTLEMAN

Ned Kelly was a gentleman: many hardships did he endure.
He battled to deprive the rich then gave it to the poor.
But his mode of distribution was not acceptable to all,
Though backed by certain gunmen known as Gilbert and Ben Hall.

I think it was a pity they hanged him from a rope;
They made Australian history but they shattered Kelly's hope.
If they'd sent him into Parliament his prospects would be bright,
He'd function for the masses if not for the elite.

And perhaps now in Australia we'd have millions trained with him,
All laughing with a vengeance at the little yellow men.
If Ned and such guerillas were here with us today
The Japs would not be prowling round New Guinea and Milne Bay.

Since Ned went over the Border there has been many a change,
Yet we may adopt his tactics around the Owen Stanley Range.
Poor Ned, he was a gentleman but never understood.
We want men of such mettle now to stem the yellow flood.[5]

And so Ned Kelly's mythic status as a national figure was secured. He has been an Australian 'man for all seasons' and the conjunction

CAR STICKER

(KELLY CENTENARY COMMITTEE)

of various important ideals in the figure of Ned Kelly has led to the creation of a national image that bears some relation to the man himself — perhaps about the same resemblance as Ned Kelly's armour had to the plough mouldboards from which it was beaten. The mask Ned Kelly has worn for more than a century has been forged from the Australian Legend, the symbol of what many have believed to be the ideal Australian. That may not be a very welcome thought in some parts of our society but the continuing enthusiasm for Ned Kelly in popular tradition leads to no other conclusion. What that tells us about Australia and the people who have made it is perhaps no more than that they like the outdoor life and are averse to unfair play; after all, bandit heroes are found in every country. But in Australia, a bandit is the *only* hero we have, at least on the national scale.

When Clive Turnbull compiled his bibliography of Kellyana in 1943 he thought that books about Ned Kelly would continue to be written 'until someone . . . has said all that remains to be said'. A worthwhile thought but an impossible task. No one will ever say all there is to be said about Ned Kelly because there will never be a final, definitive Ned Kelly. He is different things to different people — a murderer, an Australian Robin Hood, a social bandit, a revolutionary leader, even a commercial commodity. But to most of us he is somehow essentially Australian. We have even been known to describe ourselves as 'Neds' to our bemused British and American cousins. Ned Kelly has secured the national pedestal because the image that we have made him in has been

our own. As long as most Australians see themselves, no matter how realistically, as tough, resourceful and independent pioneer types who give everyone a fair go but take no nonsense from anyone, Ned Kelly will endure. Perhaps we will too.

CHAPTER 10

'POOR NED, YOU'RE BETTER OFF DEAD'

N ed Kelly has endured through the years since the centenary of his execution. So have the diverse Australian peoples, even through some fundamental economic and social changes that are challenging many of the widely accepted views of our past. We have continued to variously, often simultaneously, celebrate, commemorate and denigrate the bushranger and his many meanings. Novelists, historians, folklorists, folksingers, judges, advertisers, film-makers, tourism promoters and producers of theatrical spectacle have not ceased from the ongoing need to render and rework the history and mythology of Ned Kelly. Librarians, curators and even politicians continue to pick over the relics of the skull, the armour and the recently re-discovered Jerilderie Letter itself.

The refusal of Ned Kelly to lie down and die was highlighted during the Sydney Olympic Games ceremonies in late 2000. Essential to Nigel Jamieson's 'Tin Symphony' segment of the opening ceremony was a number of Ned Kelly representations. With Nolanesque 'heads' and draped in black rain-capes, these light-hearted but faintly disturbing figures armed with pyrotechnic rifles escorted a parade of Australian icons through Olympic Park.[1] This spectacle dramatically announced that our enigmatic national hero was back on centre stage, along with the water tanks and the other 'Australian' objects we chose to show to the world. What the world made of it can only be imagined. But a great

147

many Australians knew what it meant. As *The Australian*'s Arts Editor Katrina Strickland noted in her account of the ceremony, titled 'Kelly Rides Again, with Nod to Nolan': 'While Australians undoubtedly would have understood last night's Kelly-Nolan references, it is less clear whether the international visitors attending the opening ceremony would have picked it all up.' Jamieson was clear about Kelly's significance, though. He was quoted in the same article saying, 'Ned Kelly is probably our most famous icon so he must represent something about us — he's a sort of Robin Hood of our culture.'[2]

Barely were the Olympics over when novelist Peter Carey launched his *True History of the Kelly Gang* (which has since been awarded the prestigious Booker Prize), a 400-page fictional cogitation by the bushranger in the style of his 'Jerilderie Letter', inspired to a considerable extent by Ian Jones' acclaimed *Ned Kelly: A Short Life* and also by Carey's abiding, if now expatriate, fascination with Australian mythology. Also in 2000, a year that will stand out in the Kelly legend, the original Jerilderie Letter mysteriously re-appeared. An anonymous donor presented it to Museum Victoria, where it is displayed today. The text of this fundamental Kelly relic can now be downloaded from the State Library of Victoria's website by anyone with a computer, a modem and an internet service provider.[3]

Carey's contribution to the Kelly story and its durable mythology is but the latest and most attention-getting of many made by Australian creative artists. Jean Bedford published *Sister Kate* in 1982 using Ned's youngest sister Kate as the central character.[4] A decade later Robert Drewe published *Our Sunshine*, an imaginative reworking of the history and mythology surrounding the Kellys.[5] A number of children's books based on the Kelly story have been published, along with tourist guides to the Kelly country and a host of self-published celebrations or eviscerations of the outlaw, in book form and also on the World Wide Web.[6] Aforementioned Kelly scholar and film-maker Ian Jones directed the TV mini-series *The Last Outlaw* in 1980 and also made important contributions to knowledge and understanding of the internal relationships of the Kellys and their supporters in his 1992 book, *The Friendship that Destroyed Ned Kelly: Joe Byrne and Aaron Sherritt*. As well as its scholarship, this book was remarkable for reproducing some facsimile pages of Ned Kelly's 'Jerilderie Letter', long believed lost to the world and previously known only in copies of varying accuracy.[7]

Popular culture treatments of the bushranger have included productions like the Yahoo Serious film, *Reckless Kelly* (1993), a zany treatment of the Kelly story that revolves around the bushranger's Robin Hood characteristics, updated, satirised and sanitised. The multi-skilled Yahoo (writer, director, co-producer, star, stuntman, etc.) presented a powerfully nationalistic retelling of the Kelly story, a kind of 1990s *Crocodile Dundee* aimed as much at the American as at the local market. American and Australian film producers obviously believed the subject of Ned, suitably retooled, was worth twenty millions of their dollars. Despite this offshore funding (something of a contradiction given the film's attitude towards foreign investment in Australia), the only occasionally crass and sometimes clever *Reckless Kelly* made some reasonably serious points about Australian culture and economics. The film ends with the bushranger/bank-robber and his 'Australian' values triumphant and with a dedication to Ned Kelly, the 'larrikin' fighter against oppression and injustice.

In February 2000 it was announced that yet another feature film about our tenacious outlaw would be shot in the Kelly country later that year. Said to have a budget of 13 million dollars and to star Greek-Australian actor Alex Dimitriades, the film is to be funded by the Australian government and a German company. At the time of writing no more has been heard of this production. However, it is also reported that Irish director Neil Jordan has acquired the film rights to Carey's best-selling Kelly novel, and Robert Drewe's *Our Sunshine* is also now in screenplay form, so cinema-goers may be regaled with a number of new Kelly films in the near future.

We have continued to talk about Ned Kelly in many ways, with even the legalities of his trial being the subject of often considerable investigation and explication. A leading legal authority has examined the bushranger's legal examination under the then-Chief Justice of Victoria, Sir Redmond Barry. In his book *The Trial of Ned Kelly*, John H. Phillips, a Supreme Court Judge, concludes that Barry's summing up to the jury in Kelly's trial

> ... would have effectively removed from the jury's consideration the issue central to Kelly's defence. Sir Redmond should have told the jury that it was for them to decide whether the police [at Stringybark Creek] were acting as ministers of justice or summary executioners

and then reviewed for the jurors the evidence relevant to this issue. Instead the matter was put to the jury in terms that were conclusive in favour of the Prosecution.

Phillips goes on to write:

Accordingly, the conclusion is inescapable that Edward Kelly was not afforded a trial according to law. Whether the result would have been any different had the jury been correctly directed is, of course, entirely another matter.[8]

Phillips shows the extent to which the Victorian establishment of the time was prepared to go in order to dispose of Kelly and the very real threat they believed he and his sympathisers might pose to social order. The magnitude of the rewards offered for Kelly's capture during 1878–80 and the extent of the armoury the Victoria Police brought to bear at Glenrowan also indicate the fear the Kelly outbreak engendered among 'the respectable classes' of Victorian society.

While the Phillips analysis of Kelly's trial adds to the lustre of Ned as oppressed avenger of his class, historian Bob Reece has thrown in a touch of iconclasm. Reece conducted extensive research into the Irish background of Ned's father, John 'Red' Kelly. He discovered that far from having been transported for a 'social' crime of an honourable kind — stealing from an English landlord as folklore had it — Ned Kelly's father was known to the police as 'a notorious character' and probably involved in the organised theft of animals from his neighbours. And, as if that were not bad enough from a myth-making perspective, Ned Kelly's father was a police informer and, quite possibly, an *agent provocateur*.[9]

Other historians and writers, such as Dagmar Balcarek, have tracked down further threads of history and legend in the Kelly story, including the remarkable characteristics of the Kelly women — Kate, Maggie and especially Ellen Kelly, mother of Ned and the rest of the brood.[10] John Molony has given us an interestingly imaginative biography of Ned, originally titled *I Am Ned Kelly*, since republished as simply *Ned Kelly*.[11] Melbourne University Press has reissued in paperback John McQuilton's classic account of the Kellys, *The Kelly Outbreak*, originally published in 1979.[12] As noted, that most indefatigable and knowledgeable of Kelly scholars, Ian Jones, has written a number of significant studies of Kelly history and biography and continues to comment on the outlaw in various public forums and debates.[13]

As well as such formal products of the culture industries, the informal and unofficial whispers of forgery, self-deception and wishful thinking have persisted through the last few decades. Various documents relating to Kelly are in circulation, including a death certificate signed by Redmond Barry. Although this has been authenticated by at least one official expert, Kelly scholars remain dubious. In 1988 the Australian Bicentennial Authority's grand travelling circus of Australian icons included what was alleged to be Ned Kelly's armour as one of its essential commodities. The armour was displayed in a caravan. This suit of armour had been exhibited in the foyer of a Sydney bank in the early 1980s. Neither of these displays was the genuine article. Since then, yet another suit of armour has been authenticated and given its 'fifteen minutes' by the media.

The saga of the Kelly gang's armour is worthy of a book in itself. The original objects were souvenired by various of the victors at Glenrowan and have turned up, or not, at different times and places since, usually surrounded with discreet silences about their 'owners'. Kelly's suit has special significance and has taken on the aura of a holy relic. The State Library of Victoria possesses the treasures of Kelly's helmet, breastplate and front apron. The other pieces are scattered through other museums, including the Police Museum and Museum Victoria. Said to be smeared with the outlaw's blood, the shoulder-guard has mysteriously surfaced again. In 2000 it was offered for sale. The State Library wanted it to complete their suit but the price — reputedly $200, 000 — was too high. By May the following year it looked as though the shoulder-guard would go to an overseas buyer. Federal Arts Minister and National Party member Peter McGuaran, invoked the rarely used Moveable Cultural Heritage Act to keep Ned's relic in Australia.

The actions and expressions of the players involved in these events nicely reflect our ambivalence about Ned Kelly. McGuaran was quoted as saying that he was 'unsympathetic' to Kelly but saw his actions at Glenrowan as 'brave', if 'futile'. The Chief Executive of the State Library of Victoria was quoted to the effect that she thought Kelly a 'villain' but was anxious to obtain the missing shoulder-guard in order to reassemble the full original suit of armour.[14] While Ned Kelly was 'bad' it is considered vital to preserve and present the pre-eminent symbols of his villainy to the Australian people.[15] In July 2001, the shoulder-plate was auctioned for $170,000, plus costs and GST. The State Library of Victoria, assisted by an undisclosed sum of federal government heritage funding, secured this piece of the bushranger's ironware. The Library is reportedly keen to extend its collection of Kelly armour.[16]

Perhaps the most intriguing tales of Ned's relics surround the mysterious theft of his skull, an event that took place in 1978 (see above). A noted Kelly historian has publicly stated that in the late 1970s he visited Old Melbourne Gaol, where one of the main tourist attractions was the skull of the bushranger. After Ned's hanging, the head was cut from the body for 'scientific purposes' related to the then-current theories of criminality and physiognomy. After its use in this manner, the skull had been kept in the gaol for decades, finally going on display in 1972. The historian, a Roman Catholic, was horrified at the sacrilege involved, and expressed his concern to one of the attendants at the gaol. Some time later, the attendant contacted the historian, telling him that he had something for him. It was, of course, Ned's skull. The amazed historian obligingly arranged for the remains to be buried in appropriately consecrated ground — somewhere.

This account has, in proper folkloric manner, been contradicted a number of times with alternate versions claiming, variously, that one or another persons has Ned's skull in his or her possession. In July and August 1999, a West Australian man claimed to be the 'custodian' of the cranium and wrote a lengthy letter lauding the outlaw, proposing that he have a 'proper burial' as a 'national figure' and asking that the bushranger be recognised as 'a father of the Australian republic'.[17] In August 2000, the keeper of Ned's skull announced that it was to be decently interred at a private ceremony with descendants of the Kellys.[18] Needless to add, perhaps, that the authenticity of this relic has been questioned.

And there are other tales to tell. Given the folkloric belief that Dan Kelly was not killed at Glenrowan but escaped to South Africa, America or wherever, it has even been claimed that it was not Ned hanged in 1880, but younger brother, Dan. It is not simply that such a delusion can exist somewhere among some nineteen-or-so million of us that highlights Ned's continuing importance, but the fact that the media rushed to get these claims on air for us all to share. This gave the allegations at least a fleeting credibility and may yet, in time, weave another strand into the ever-expanding Kelly legend. A few years later, just as the shoulder-guard of Ned Kelly's armour was being auctioned, an amateur Kelly historian, Gary J. Deane, proprietor of Glenrowan's Ned Kelly Museum, announced his intention to prove that Dan and Steve Hart did not die at Glenrowan. He aimed to support his claim by exhuming a body buried in Queensland and comparing its DNA with a sample of hair given to him by a female Kelly descendant.[19] At the time of writing nothing further had been heard of this intriguing attempt to authenticate folklore.

Even though Ned's — or someone else's — mortal remains have been laid to rest, there is no sign of the Kelly legend dying. Lawyers, historians, film-makers, novelists and journalists continue to approach Ned Kelly, his story and his folklore, in a variety of ways. Ned, like the saint that Keith Dunstan titled him, has his hagiographers, his mythologists, his forgers, his fakers, his salespeople and, apparently, even his would-be saviours. Nor should we overlook the material homages to the national icon, the mailboxes, concrete garden statuary and key-rings that trade on the bushranger's image. These are just some of the endlessly ingenious ways we have found to reify our Ned. Need a national hero, an Australian myth, provide any further evidence of his sanctification and commodification?

But is Ned Kelly relevant to the new Australia? Can Aboriginal people, for instance, identify with an Anglo-Celtic bushranger? It seems that Ned Kelly has developed connections with indigenous people. Descendants of some of the Aboriginal trackers who worked with the police during the Kelly hunt, Wannamutta, also known as Jack Noble, and Werannabe, known as 'Barney' or Gary Owens, are now claiming their share of the reward — fifty pounds plus a lot of interest and damages. The total under claim from the Victorian government by February 1997 had reached over $80 million.[20] In the Northern Territory, Aborigines have adopted Kelly into their cultures, in some cases significantly conflated with Jesus Christ, other biblical figures and Captain Cook.[21] Ned's defiance of duly constituted authority and his insistence on the repressive nature of government and police has caused some West Australian Aborigines to see Kelly as an appropriate representative of their own grievances and struggle.

It is this Robin Hood element of the bushranger that may also resonate with Australians from backgrounds other than Anglo–Celtic. Kelly is the epitome of the Australian branch of an international 'noble robber' tradition. Many readers may be familiar with the English-language manifestations of this tradition, including British highway-men Dick Turpin, Claude Duval and American badmen like Jesse James and Sam Bass. But the noble robber or 'Robin Hood' figure who re-dresses the political and economic wrongs done to the poor by the rich and powerful, is a cultural constant throughout the world, appearing in many guises in many nationalities.[22] Ned Kelly's struggle and his mythology are the antipodean variant of an international folk tradi-tion that is meaningful to Australians whose cultural antecedents are not those of the British Isles. These factors suggest that Ned Kelly's extensive legendry will survive well into the new millennium.

Based on the last 120 years of Kelly conversation, Ned has serious staying power as our leading national icon. Back in the 1970s when I began researching Ned Kelly people told me, very seriously and often with a figurative wag of the finger, that Ned Kelly was no longer rele-vant to the Australian people and that he would be relegated to the dustbins of history and myth long before the end of the century. These people were genuine, if now clearly wrong — Ned Kelly continues to occupy his unique position in Australian culture. But *why* has Ned Kelly persisted in the national consciousness for so long?

His image as a bush Robin Hood is part of the answer. The gen-eral figure of the bushranger focuses some of our most cherished and persistent myths. These include our fascination with those who defy authority, especially if the authority wears a uniform and the defying is done from a position of powerlessness. This automatically makes them a 'battler' and Ned becomes the underdog who bites back on behalf of us all. It is clear that Kelly was keenly aware of these matters and went to some lengths to present himself and his actions accordingly. He addressed large crowds at his various bank robberies and occupa-tions. He wrote, or dictated, two letters that indicate his understand-ing of the tradition in which he worked. These expressed his and, more importantly, his sympathisers' anger at what they perceived to be their unjust treatment by the Victorian government, police and the squat-ters who had occupied the best land in the area a generation or so before the free selecting Kellys and their like arrived.

The location of Ned Kelly's story in the bush is an important contribution to the bushranger's continued appeal. This taps into one of our more powerful cultural traditions that locates those things felt to be uniquely and characteristically 'Australian' in the rural regions. By contrast the city is seen as the location of negative elements. It is full of poverty, despair, moral decay and generally imposes intolerable burdens of responsibility on those of us who must live there. As often pointed out, that is the vast majority of us, a fact that at least partly accounts for our longing for escape, even if mostly vicariously, to the bush.

There are countless literary and folkloric expressions that operate on these same assumptions.[23] This negative depiction of the urban, always explicitly or implicitly contrasted with and opposed to the freedom and cultural authenticity of the bush, is a pivotal concern in Australian mythology and has been so for over a century. In such a post-Romantic arcadianism, the fact that Ned Kelly defied authority, fought against oppression and was on the side of 'the bush battlers', as made abundantly clear in his Jerilderie and Cameron Letters, has substantially assisted his rise to heroism. The fact that his trial and execution were in the city and that his death was formally pronounced by a solid member of the establishment, Judge Redmond Barry, neatly focused this fundamental opposition within Australian culture and allowed the lustre of Ned Kelly, the man who ranged the bush, to shine even more brightly in death than in life.

The tension manifested so electrically between the judge and the bushranger was another expression of the long troubles between England and Ireland and their echoes in Australia. Kelly's 'Irishness' represented all that the English establishment feared and despised in the Celtic culture they had colonised and oppressed for centuries. The large numbers of Irish and Irish-descended people in Australia always meant that these feared 'others' were constantly eyeball-to-eyeball with an often abrasively English system of government and policing. Kelly's Irishness has been a powerful element of his legendry and one that has continued to fuel the Irish claim to a place in the Australian sun.[24] Tensions of this sort have abated as the Irish have consolidated their presence throughout Australian culture and society. Irishness is now an accepted element of the national mythology, its past dissonances mediated and romanticised through notions of 'cultural heritage' and the marketing of a famous Irish beverage. As part of the Centenary of

Federation celebrations, Irish Post issued a set of postage stamps on the theme of Irish Heritage in Australia. These unerringly represented the fundamentals of Australian Irishness — Australia the Land of Promise, the rebel spirit of the Eureka Stockade and, inevitably, Ned Kelly. The Melbourne Celtic Club, partly sponsored by Guinness, mounted an elaborate night of talk, music, song and general celebration on 3 May, 2001.[25]

That year also saw the first of what will surely be a number of publications dealing with the outlaw's recently rediscovered correspondence. Alex McDermott's *The Jerilderie Letter* calls Kelly's statement an 'apocalyptic chant', deliberately suggesting a link with the blood-soaked novel and subsequent film *The Chant of Jimmie Blacksmith*.[26] For McDermott, following the Manning Clark view of Kelly as a 'satanic thug', Kelly is a terrorising butcher and the Jerilderie Letter an attempt to intimidate and dominate. 'The letter leaves us with a very different impression of Ned Kelly from the one we are usually given. It tells the story of a violent man leading a violent life...'.

McDermott is correct. Kelly was a terrorist and his letter seeks to terrorise. But Ned Kelly was also much more than that and the Jerilderie Letter a far more complex document than McDermott's narrow interpretation allows. The Jerilderie Letter is in the lengthy tradition of the threatening letters scrawled by agricultural labourers driven to the desperation of revolt by the rational rural capitalism of eighteenth and nineteenth century England and Wales and the worse privations of the Irish. Its threats are largely incantatory, though they have serious intent.[27] Kelly's words, written down by Joe Byrne, go far beyond the genre of the threatening letter, though, articulating something of a political philosophy, chronicling his life and that of those like him and revealing the folk history of Irish convictism. To reduce this savagely colourful, often humorous and passionate outpouring to a mere threatening letter is to wilfully ignore its cultural context and its rich intertextuality.

Negative or positive, this continued interest in Kelly and his mythology by writers, historians, film-makers, advertisers[28] and other creative artists suggests that he still has a potent place in Australian folk and popular culture. It also suggests that the cultural traditions he represents still have a grip on national identity. The bush, its pioneering, the class conflict over land and resources, attitudes towards the forces of authority, the egalitarian notion of the 'fair go' are all integral elements of Ned Kelly's image. His enigmatic aura and ambivalence — the focus of Nolan's artistic depictions — are also powerful elements of Australian identity.[29] Ned Kelly's ability to simultaneously signify both positive and negative elements of our history and folklore and to continually mediate and negotiate them is characteristic of Australia's other most powerful mythology, that of Anzac and the Digger. Anzac Day, still 'the one day of the year', temporarily displays the contradictions of the invented Anzac tradition of militarism, sacrifice and national duty and the spontaneous folk traditions that produced the iconic figure of the digger with his larrikinism, his drinking and irreverence.

There are profound contradictions within and around both these icons of nation, contradictions that go to the centre of the great Australian emptiness. Still 'second-hand Europeans' clustering nervously around 'alien shores' as A.D. Hope discerned many years ago, our tentative status made even more tenuous by the revelations of profound historical wrongs inflicted on those who lived upon the land for so long before Europeans occupied it. Our quest for national identity is reflected in the adoption of figures such as Ned Kelly and the digger whose ambivalences at once express our contradictions, our uncertainties and resolve them — at least for a while.

The elevation of a bushman who robbed banks and murdered policemen to the status of national hero represents our need to balance often mutually opposing notions that reflect our national uncertainty. In Kelly's day it was the uncertainty of ethnicity: Redmond Barry's Englishness as the dominant mode of identity versus Kelly's dangerous Irish–Australianism. In World War 1 we once again grappled with the problem of whether we were British or 'Australian'. We did not resolve that issue but again settled for a schizoid dual identity of being British–Australians. After World War 2 the influx of migrants from non-Anglo-Saxon backgrounds once again threw us into an identity crisis. At first we tried to make them as much like us as quickly as possible. We failed and developed multiculturalism, another consensus that has — so far — nicely balanced a great many competing and conflicting cultural tensions. Since the floating of the dollar in 1983 Australians have been increasingly exposed to the cold winds of economic rationalism and globalisation, undermining the old certainties for many. Pauline Hanson and One Nation were the emotional political response to these pressures, another characteristic attempt to balance old and new Australia, past romance and present reality.

As well as possessing the ability to mediate such contradictions, the bush Robin Hood, the armoured outlaw vainly but valiantly defying the forces of the state, is a powerful metaphor of resistance to the kind of change that many Australians feel is beyond their control and overwhelming their previously secure assumptions. The ungraspable, intangible but, for many, devastating forces of economic and social change operate on a global scale but impact locally. To those who supported and sympathised with Ned Kelly and his companions the forces of the state, the banks and the squatters were just as unavoidable. Ned Kelly's image still has the ability to link these resistant situations across time and space. The past, no matter how mythologised, speaks to the present through the submerged, unremarked but nevertheless potent forces of popular tradition.

In the Foreword to the original edition of this book Russel Ward linked Ned Kelly, the Anzac tradition of the two world wars and the political events of 1975. He correctly perceived their connections with the national mythology, 'The Australian Legend' as he memorably called it in his famous book of that name. While Ward's rendering of 'the legend' has been rightly criticised as too celebratory, male-oriented and Anglo-centric, his insight into the fundamental mythology of modern Australia remains essentially intact. Many, perhaps most, Australians continue to identify with the legend, oblivious to or uncaring of its racism, its sexism and its jingoism. Whenever there is a need to signify 'nation', as in Bicentennial, Olympic and Federation Centennial celebrations we reach for those tried and true icons of the bush, the digger and Ned Kelly. Much as the literate, the elevated and the politically correct might regret and reject such vulgar clichés of nation, they persist and resound again and again in what Australians say.

Ned Kelly was one of the cut-out models in the Peoplescapes Centenary of Federation art project. Funded with 2.8 millions of taxpayers' dollars, Ned was one of 5000 Australians chosen for this piece of Canberra installation art. Those chosen for this honour were suggested by members of the public. The man who nominated our Ned was Melburnian Robert Jan. Describing himself as 'a very ordinary person', Mr Jan was quoted as saying he nominated Ned Kelly because 'I knew everyone else would suggest saints and fine, upstanding people leaving historical figures like Ned Kelly out. He may have been a convicted criminal, but he had a big impact on Australian culture.[30] Mr Jan was dead right. The rediscovery of Ned Kelly, like the rediscovery of Republicanism that immediately preceded it,[31] is persuasive evidence of the continuing appeal of this version of our past. The question now is whether this popular past will continue to sustain our need for national identity through the inevitable changes of the twenty-first century.

If the federal government's publicity for its centenary of federation activities in 2001 was any indication, it seems that Ned Kelly is likely to remain our favourite national symbol for some time to come. Expensive colour advertisements in Australian newspapers during September 2001 were dominated by a striking Nolan image of the bushranger, mounted and armed, a detail from the 1946 *Kelly and Horse* painting. The caption asked the provocative question: 'What kind of country would make a bushranger a cultural icon?' No answers were provided. Instead, a brief outline of Australian cultural history since 1901 was offered, including Mel Gibson in his outlaw role as Mad Max. The text made two further references to Ned Kelly — the 1906 feature film and Nolan's Kelly series. Once again, Ned was ahead on points as the dominant figure of our cultural mythology.

The lyrics of the late Trevor Lucas's well-known 'Poor Ned' providing the title of this chapter suggest that, in death, Ned will at least 'get some peace of mind'. The composer makes a direct link between Jesus Christ and Ned Kelly: 'Well, I don't know what's right or wrong, but they hung Christ on nails ...'[32] Effectively rebutting Manning Clarke's patrician view of Kelly as a 'satanic thug' Lucas, drawing on folk traditions and continuing attitudes, provides an updated rendition — yet another — of the Kelly legend. Patrician villain, plebeian hero, Ned is neither one or the other. His image persists in the national consciousness because he is both these things, and much more besides. Ned Kelly the man is 'better off dead'. Ned Kelly the folk hero, media hero and national hero will, like it or not, live in our legendry for a long time.

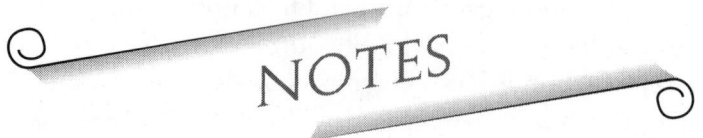

CHAPTER 1: Introduction

1 See R. Ward, *The Australian Legend* (London, 1958); K. Inglis, 'The Anzac Tradition', *Meanjin* (1965), vol. 24, no. 1; T. Inglis Moore, 'The Meaning of Mateship', ibid.; G. Serle, 'The Digger Tradition and Australian Nationalism', ibid., no. 2, for some indications of the growth and development of the rural myth in Australia.

2 G. Wilson Hall, *The Kelly Gang, or the Outlaws of the Wombat Ranges* (Mansfield, Vic., 1879).

3 D. Stewart and N. Keesing, *Old Bush Songs* (Sydney, 1957), p. 45, from J. Small's *Colonial Songster*.

4 *Songs of the Kelly Gang* (Hobart, ?1879; Mitchell Library: 784.4/12).

CHAPTER 2: Highwaymen, outlaws and bushrangers

1 Collected by Ron Edwards from the singing of Mrs K. Andreau (Qld), in R. Edwards, *The Big Book of Australian Folk Songs* (Sydney, 1976), p. 254.

2 Ned Kelly, Jerilderie Letter.

3 E. J. Hobsbawm, *Bandits* (London, 1969). See also W. E. Simeone, 'Robin Hood and Some Other Outlaws', *Journal of American Folklore*, 71 (1958); O. Klapp, 'The Folk Hero', ibid., 62 (1949); E. Stenbock-Fermor, 'The Story of Van'ka Kain', in A. Lord (ed.), *Slavic Folklore: A Symposium* (Philadelphia, 1956).

4 F. J. Child, *The English and Scottish Popular Ballads*, 5 vols (1882–1908; New York, 1965), vol. 3, pp. 42–3.

5 Broadside printed by J. M. Robertson (Glasgow, Saltmarket, 1803; British Library 11606 aa 23), spelling and punctuation modernised.

6 Collected from Mrs M. Bradley, in F. Hamer, *Garners Gay* (London, 1967), p. 6.

7 Broadside printed by C. Such (1865), in *The Chapbook*, No. 15 (Sept. 1920), p. 22. See also Newman Ivey White, Paull F. Baum, et al. (eds), *The Frank C. Brown Collection of North Carolina Folklore*, 6 vols (Durham, N.C., 1952–), vol. 2, pp. 356–7, for an American oral version.

8 P. O'Shaughnessy (ed.), *Yellowbelly Ballads*, Part 1 (Lincoln, 1975), pp. 9–10, taken from C. J. Ingledew, *The Ballads and Songs of Yorkshire* (London, 1860), pp. 125–8. See also C. Hindley, *Curiosities of Street Literature* (London, 1871), p. 169.

9 Collected in Somerset by Cecil Sharp, 1903, in M. Karpeles (ed.), *Cecil Sharp's Collection of English Folk Songs* (London, 1974), vol. 2, pp. 166–7.

10 For instance, 'The Highwayman' in F. Kidson, *A Garland of English Folksong* (London, 1926), pp. 96–7; 'The Flying Highwayman', in J. Holloway and J. Black (eds), *Later English Broadside Ballads* (London, 1975), pp. 104–5.

11 A. L. Hayward (ed.), *Lives of the Most Remarkable Criminals* (1735; London, 1927), p. 57; also pp. 111–12.

12 M. Larkin, *The Singing Cowboy* (New York, 1931), and printed in B. Botkin (ed.), *A Treasury of American Folklore* (New York, 1944), p. 108.

13 'Song of Billy the Kid' in J. and A. Lomax (eds), *American Ballads and Folksongs* (New York, 1934), pp. 137–8; 'Sam Bass', in R. Lingenfelter et al. (eds), *Songs of the American West* (Los Angeles, 1968), pp. 316–17; 'Quantrell', in ibid., pp. 314–15. See also a song called 'Jim Fisk' in H. M. Belden (ed.), *Ballads and Songs Collected by the Missouri Folklore Society* (Columbia, 1940), pp. 415–16.

14 R. Lingenfelter, op. cit., p. 235.

15 Public Records Office, London, Colonial Office Papers, CO 201/89F 128v.

16 Quoted in C. White, *History of Australian Bushranging* 2 vols (1975 edn), vol. 1, p. 43.

17 Ibid., pp.76–7.

18 J. Bonwick, *The Bushrangers: Illustrating The Early History of Tasmania* '(Melbourne, 1856), p. 89.

19 See J. Manifold, *Who Wrote The Ballads: Notes on Australian Folksong* (Sydney, 1964), pp. 21–41, 42–7; and J. Meredith, *The Wild Colonial Boy: The Life and Times of Jack Donahue, 1808-1830* (Sydney, 1960).

20 *Northern Folk*, No. 17 (Sept. 1967), p. 9.

21 D. Stewart and N. Keesing, *Australian Bush Ballads* (Melbourne, 1955), pp. 34-5. See also M. Carnegie, *Morgan—The Bold Bushranger* (Melbourne, 1974).

22 B. Tate, 'The Fate of Thunderbolt', *Stringybark and Greenhide,* vol. 2, no. 2 (April 1980).

23 Quoted in G. Boxall, *History of the Australian Bushrangers* (Sydney, 1935), pp. 200–1.

24 *Sydney Morning Herald,* 26 Feb. 1863.

25 This text is a reconstruction based on two versions, one in J. Bradshaw, *The Only True Account of Ned Kelly, Frank Gardiner, Ben Hall and Morgan* (Sydney, 1911), p. 6, and from the singing of Mrs Popplewell in J. Meredith and H. Anderson, *Folksongs of Australia* (Melbourne, 1967; 1973), p. 30.

26 Collected by John Meredith from Mrs Gladys Scrivener, c. 1950s, in Meredith and Anderson, op. cit., pp. 98–9. For more oral traditions about Ben Hall and other bushrangers see my *The Highwayman Tradition in Australia* (Folklore Occasional Paper No. 9, Sydney, 1977).

27 Jerilderie Letter.

CHAPTER 3: 'Fearless, free and bold'

1 See F. Hare, *The Last of the Bushrangers* (London, 1892).

2 See J. McQuilton, *The Kelly Outbreak, 1878–1880: The Geographical Dimension of Social Banditry* (Melbourne, 1979), pp. 196–8.

3 See J. Powell (ed.), *Yeomen and Bureaucrats: The Victorian Crown Lands Commission, 1878–9* (London, 1973). See also *Argus,* 4 March 1878, for editorial on exorbitance of land tax, particularly in Benalla; J. McQuilton, op. cit., chs 3–5.

4 W. Bate, 'Ned Kelly and His Times', C. Cave (ed.), *Ned Kelly: Man and Myth* (Sydney, 1968), pp. 40ff.; and McQuilton, op. cit., ch. 2.

5 J. Sadleir, *Recollections of a Victorian Police Officer* (1913; Penguin facsimile, 1973), pp. 65–7; T. O'Callaghan, 'Police in Port Phillip and Victoria, 1836–1913', *Victorian*

Historical Magazine, No. 4, (June 1928); and W. Burrows, *Adventures of a Mounted Trooper in the Australian Constabulary* (London, 1859), pp. 23–5, 45–8.

6 See H. King, 'Some Aspects of Police Administration in New South Wales, 1825–51', in *Journal of the Royal Australian Historical Society*, vol. 42, pt 5 (1956); T. O'Callaghan, 'Police Establishment in New South Wales', ibid., vol. 9, pt 6, (1923); and M. Brennan, 'A Police History of the Notorious Bushrangers of New South Wales and Victoria' (MS., Mitchell Library: A2030).

7 *Royal Commission on the Police Force of Victoria 1881*, Minutes of Evidence, Questions 15488–15493, 15797–15800, 17566 (hereafter *PC*; published in facsimile, Adelaide, 1969).

8 Ibid., pp. 719–20.

9 Police inadequacies, often noted by the Victorian press during the Kelly period (see *Age*, 2 Nov. 1878, 7 Feb. 1879; and *Argus* 8 Nov. 1879, p. 7, for example), were not novel; see G. Wathan, *The Golden Colony of Victoria in 1854* (London, 1855), pp. 142, 179–82; and R. Henty, *Australiana, or My Early Life* (London, 1886), p. 183. Also D. Chappell and P. Wilson, *The Police and the People in Australia and New Zealand* (St Lucia, Qld, 1969), pp. 28ff.

10 This was how Ned Kelly saw the situation in his Cameron and Jerilderie Letters. See also J. J. Kenneally, *The Complete Inner History of the Kelly Gang* (Moe, Vic., 1929).

11 J. Powell, op. cit., Questions 8723–8726. See J. McQuilton, op. cit., pp. 48–56.

12 Barbour rented 5000 acres and had purchased 2000 more.

13 *PC*, Appendix 1, pp. 679–82, Question 29.

14 See Montford's other evidence of criminality in the Kelly country, ibid., Questions 3237–3559; also I. Jones, 'A New View of Ned Kelly', in Cave, op. cit., pp. 154–89.

15 See J. Powell, op. cit., passim; for contemporary expressions of discontent see *Age*, 7 Nov. 1878 (editorial), 10 Dec. 1878 (letter); and *Argus*, 14 March 1878 (letter), 1 Nov. 1878 (editorial and letter), 8 Nov. 1878 (letter).

16 *PC*, QQ. 1024 ff.

17 J. McQuilton, op. cit., pp. 70–90.

CHAPTER 4: 'What a bloody pity the bastard tried to run'

1 *PC*, QQ. 12801–12994. Mrs Kelly married George King in February 1874 but it is convenient to continue to refer to her as Mrs Kelly.

2 Ibid., Q. 13440, evidence of W. Foster, local police magistrate.

3 J. McQuilton, *The Kelly Outbreak, 1878–1880: The Geographical Dimension of Social Banditry* (Melbourne, 1979), p. 96.

4 *PC*, QQ. 14319–14414, evidence of Const. McIntyre; and McQuilton, op. cit., pp. 95–7.

5 *Felon's Apprehension Act, Victoria, 1878*.

6 Collected by Rev. Dr Percy Jones, in C. Cave (ed.), *Ned Kelly: Man and Myth* (Sydney, 1968), pp. 84–5. This first appears in G. Wilson Hall, *The Kelly Gang, or the Outlaws of the Wombat Ranges* (Mansfield, Vic., 1879), to the tune of 'Going to Ballarat'.

7 *Argus*, 16 Dec. 1878 (editorial).

8 *PC*, Q. 1393, 3136–3154.

9 Ibid., QQ. 2054–2067.

10 Ibid.

11 Ibid., QQ. 2390, 12528–12538, 3833, 12181–12188, 14550–14556.

12 See ibid., QQ. 1865–6; McQuilton, op. cit., pp. 96, 100.

13 *New South Wales Public Statutes*, 1 Geo. IV, No. X.

14 *Historical Records of Australia*, Series 1, vol. 17, pp. 520–36.

15 *New South Wales Public Statutes*, 28 Vic., No. 2.

16 *Sydney Morning Herald*, 17 May 1865 (editorial).

17 *PC*, QQ. 1365–1368, 2382–2390, 12688–12695.
18 Ibid., QQ. 269–271, 554–558, 9380–9388.
19 Ibid., Appendix 5, pp. 690–5.
20 Ibid., QQ. 1365–1368, 1372.
21 *Argus*, 28 Feb. 1879 (editorial).
22 For instance, *Argus*, 13 Oct., 8 Nov., 13, 31 Dec. 1878; 12, 17, 28 Feb. 1879; 1, 2
    July 1880; and *Age*, 2, 19 Nov., 12, 17 Dec. 1878; 7, 12, 24 Feb. 1879; 4 Nov. 1880.
23 *Argus*, 13 Nov. 1878.
24 Ibid., 18 Dec. 1878.
25 Ibid., 28 Feb. 1879.
26 Ibid., 18 Dec. 1878.
27 Ibid., 12 Feb. 1879.
28 Ibid., 13 Nov. 1878.
29 Ibid., 6 March 1879.
30 Ibid.
31 *Age*, 17 Dec. 1878.
32 *Argus*, 16, 18 Dec. 1878.

CHAPTER 5: 'I will oppose your laws'
1 For an eye-witness account of the Euroa raid see Mrs R. Scott, 'The Kelly Gang at
    Euroa' (typescript, Mitchell Library: A4143). Mrs Scott was the wife of the Euroa
    bank manager and the lady who declared that 'Ned Kelly was a gentleman'.
2 Ibid.
3 See *Age*, 12 Dec. 1878 (editorial); 13 Dec. 1878; 7, 10 Feb. 1879; and *Argus*, 13, 16,
    18 Dec. 1878.
4 *Age*, 17 Dec. 1878.
5 G. Wilson Hall, *The Kelly Gang, or the Outlaws of the Wombat Ranges* (Mansfield,
    Vic., 1879), also in the broadsheet, *Songs of the Kelly Gang* (Hobart, ?1879; Mitchell
    Library: 784.4/12).

CHAPTER 6: 'I am a widow's son outlawed'
1 Rev. H. G Lundy, *Jerilderie: 100 Years* (Jerilderie, N.S.W., 1958), p. 71. Includes 'The
    Kelly Raid on Jerilderie by One Who Was There', written in 1913, pp. 64ff. All subse-
    quent references to Lundy are to this statement.
2 Lundy, p. 78.
3 Lundy, p. 96.
4 Lundy, pp. 76–7.
5 Lundy, pp. 85, 96, 102, 107. On the presence of 'strangers' at Jerilderie see *Age*, 21 Feb.
    1879, which states that swagmen aided the bushrangers during the raid.
6 Kelly Papers, Victorian Public Records Office.
7 Lundy, p. 105.
8 Quoted in J. McQuilton, *The Kelly Outbreak, 1878–1880: The Geographical
    Dimension of Social Banditry* (Melbourne, 1979), p. 119.
9 This statement is based on Ned Kelly's account in the Cameron and Jerilderie Letters
    and McIntyre's evidence in *PC*, QQ. 14319-14414. See also J. McQuilton, op. cit.,
    pp. 98–100.
10 See E. H. Fosbery to H. Parkes, 14 March 1879, Parkes Correspondence, vol. 13, p. 235
    (Mitchell Library: A883), and Ned Kelly's request to see his mother and sister before
    he was hanged, State Library of Victoria Archives, Melbourne. This document is written
    by a prison official and signed only with a cross. But see J. McQuilton, op. cit., p. 75,
    for evidence that the ten-year-old Ned could read and write.

11 J. Bradshaw, *Highway Robbery Under Arms (Sticking up of the Quirindi Bank and full account of Thunderbolt)* (Sydney, n.d. [1934]), p. 181. This edition of Bradshaw's book titles the ballad 'The Convicts Arrival', followed by 'On Poor Old Frank McNamara'. The first (c. 1899) edition has a slightly different text and is untitled. For the background to this song see J. Meredith and R. Whalan, *Frank The Poet* (Melbourne, 1979).
12 Jerilderie Letter.
13 Lundy, p. 119, also pp. 88–9.

CHAPTER 7: 'Some colonial stratagem'
1 In C. Cave (ed.), *Ned Kelly: Man and Myth* (Sydney, 1968), pp. 90–1.
2 *PC*, Q. 13393.
3 Ibid., Q. 13286, evidence of Aaron Sherritt's widow.4 Ibid., QQ. 7719–7729.
5 Ibid., Q. 10617, evidence of Mrs Reardon.
6 *Australasian Sketcher*, 3 July 1880, p. 147.
7 Burke Museum, Beechworth, Victoria.
8 *Argus*, 1 Nov. 1880.
9 Rev. H. C. Lundy, *Jerilderie: 100 Years* (Jerilderie, N.S.W., 1958), p. 117.
10 Collected by Max Brown from Mrs Barry, Beechworth, Victoria, in D. Stewart and N. Keesing, *Old Bush Songs* (Sydney, 1957; 1976), p. 48.

CHAPTER 8: The making of a hero
1 G. Wilson Hall, *The Kelly Gang, or the Outlaws of the Wombat Ranges* (Mansfield, Vic., 1879), pp. 108–9.
2 Verse 1 is slightly reworded from the singing of Mr Jack Luscombe, collected by John Meredith, in Meredith and Anderson, *Folksongs of Australia* (Melbourne, 1967), p. 28. Verse 2 is from Mr Cyril Duncan, collected by Warren Fahey in 1973, and Verse 3 appeared in the *Bulletin*, 10 June 1882.
3 Collected from Mr Cyril Duncan by Warren Fahey, 1973.
4 Collected by John Meredith and Mr W. Shawcross, in Meredith and Anderson, op. cit., pp. 203–4.
5 Collected by John Meredith from Mr T. Gibbons, in ibid., pp. 248–9.
6 *Herald* (Melbourne), 14 Nov. 1930. See *Sun News-Pictorial*, 11 Nov. 1930, for another letter on a similar theme, and *Age*, 18 April 1931, for an article by J. J. Kenneally attempting to discredit survival stories.
7 Quoted in C. Cave (ed.), *Ned Kelly: Man and Myth* (Sydney, 1968), p. 206. See p. 202 for another letter about Dan and Steve's survival.
8 *Bulletin*, 4 Oct. 1933. See also Henry H. Neary, *The Kellys, Australia's Famous Bushrangers* (Sydney, n.d.), p. 39.
9 Quoted in D. Stewart and N. Keesing, *Australian Bush Ballads* (Sydney, 1955), pp. 48–9.
10 See, for example Ellis H. Davidson, 'Folklore and History', *Folklore*, 85 (1974), and A. Smith, 'Some Folklore Elements in Movements of Social Protest', ibid., 77 (1966).
11 *Stringybark and Greenhide*, vol. 1, no. 2 (1979), p. 18, located in the papers of Charles Noble by Brad Tate, 1971.
12 W. M. Hughes, 'Mr Hughes Tells a Tale of the Kelly Gang: A Bright Weekend in Jerilderie', *Herald* (Melbourne), 10 Jan. 1934.
13 An earlier film, made in 1905 by the Salvation Army and titled *Soldiers of the Cross,* is not generally considered to be a true 'movie'.
14 *Argus*, 15 Oct. 1934.
15 W. Fahey, *Joe Watson: Australian Traditional Folk Singer* (Folklore Occasional Paper No. 8, Sydney, 1975).

16 Tex Morton's song was called 'The Ned Kelly Song', on Regal Zonophone Catalogue No. G 23895, and Billy Blinkhorn's was called 'Poor Ned Kelly' on Regal Zonophone Catalogue No. G 23882. For further disco-graphical details of Kelly songs by other Australian country performers see E. Watson, *Country Music in Australia* (Sydney, rev. edn 1976).

17 'The Kelly Gang of Robbers', *The Banker's Magazine*, vol. 5 (Jan. 1892), pp. 352, 354.

18 C. E. Taylor, *The Girl Who Helped Ned Kelly* (Melbourne, 1929).

19 C. Hayter, *Ned Kelly: A Tale of Trooper and Bushranger* (n.d.). Most of the Kelly films also took the Hollywood 'western' approach, complete with large 'posses' thundering across the country in pursuit of the Kellys, sometimes to the accompaniment of can-can music!

20 See C. Turnbull, *Kellyana* (Melbourne, 1943), and J. McQuilton, *The Kelly Outbreak, 1878–1880: The Geographical Dimension of Social Banditry* (Melbourne, 1979), Appendix 6: 'Kelly Literature a Brief Review'.

21 See W. Wannan, *Pix*, 18 Oct. 1952, for 'The Ned Kelly Song' (a fragment) and LP disc, *The Original Bushwackers and Bullockies Bush Band*, Larrikin Record LRF 019. For the oral provenance of 'Poor Ned Kelly' see LP disc *Glenrowan To The Gulf*, EMI SOEX 9631.

22 J. S. Borlase, *Ned Kelly, The Ironclad Australian Bushranger* (London, 1881).

23 J. Kelly in J. J. Kenneally, *The Complete Inner History of The Kelly Gang and Their Pursuers* (Moe, Vic., 1929; 1945), pp. 200–1. See also Kenneally's article 'They All Died', *Age*, 18 April 1931.

24 This version from Mrs Gladys Scrivener, in Meredith and Anderson, op. cit., pp. 99–100.

25 Rev. W. H. Fitchett, *Ned Kelly and His Gang* (Melbourne, 1958), p. 6. This work began life in 1913 as part of *The New World of the South. The Romance of Australian History* and was frequently reprinted in various guises up to 1942.

26 Henry H. Neary, op. cit., p. 39.

27 See S. Baker, *The Australian Language* (1945; Melbourne, 1976).

28 Given in an unsigned letter to I. Jones in C. Cave, op. cit., p. 205.

CHAPTER 9: The continuing image of Ned Kelly

1 J. Manifold, 'The Death of Ned Kelly', *The Death of Ned Kelly and Other Ballads* (London, 1941). For 'Poor Ned', composed by Trevor Lucas, hear LP disc *If You Don't Fight You Lose* by Redgum, Larrikin Records, LRF 037, 1979. See also publications like *The Independent Australian* and *The Builders' Labourer's Song Book* (Camberwell, Vic., 1975).

2 C. Cave (ed.), *Ned Kelly: Man and Myth* (Sydney, 1968).

3 One of the reasons for the many dramatic and quasi-dramatic renditions of the Kelly story, such as the early Ned Kelly plays, Douglas Stewart's *Ned Kelly. A Play*, (Sydney and London, 1943), Robbitt Jon Clow's *The Causes of Kelly, A Complete History of the Primitive Colonial War between The Kelly Family and the Police; in blank verse* (Ballarat, Vic., 1919), and, of course, the films. There was even a Ned Kelly musical produced a few years ago and a Ned Kelly comic strip.

4 M. Brown, *Australian Son: The Story of Ned Kelly* (Melbourne, 1948), p. 206.

5 R. Ward (ed.), *The Penguin Book of Australian Bush Ballads* (Ringwood, Vic., 1964), pp. 247–8.

CHAPTER 10: 'Poor Ned, you're better off dead'

1 Jamieson's *Kelly's Republic*, enacted at the Melbourne Festival in 1996 introduced this representation of Ned Kelly, reinforced at a repeat performance before the Sydney Opera House the next year, said to have been attended by 80, 000.

2 *The Australian* Sept. 16, 2000, p. 7.

3 www.slv.vic.gov.au

4 Bedford, J., *Sister Kate*, Ringwood, 1982.

5 Drewe, R., *Our Sunshine*, Ringwood, 1992.

6 For example Powell, G., *Ned Kelly Country*, Robert Brown &Associates, 1997. There are also a number of websites devoted to Ned Kelly.

7 Jones, I., *The Friendship that Destroyed Ned Kelly: Joe Byrne and Aaron Sherritt*, Port Melbourne, 1992. A great number of self-published celebrations and condemnations of Ned Kelly have also appeared since 1980.

8 Phillips, J., *The Trial of Ned Kelly*, Sydney, 1987, p. 94.

9 Reece, R., 'Ned Kelly's Father' in Reece, R. (ed.), *Exiles from Erin: Convict Lives in Ireland and Australia*, London, 1991.

10 Balcarek, D., *Ellen Kelly*, Glenrowan, 1984.

11 Molony, J., *I Am Ned Kelly*, Ringwood, 1981.

12 McQuilton, J., *The Kelly Outbreak, 1878-1880: The Geographical Dimension of Social Banditry*, Melbourne, 1979.

13 Correspondence in *The Australian* 30 Oct. and 1 Nov., 2000 and Alex McDermott's review of a number of Kelly and related books in *Eureka Street*, Jan.–Feb. 2001 and subsequent ABC-TV *Lateline* program debate. See also an article by Cameron Stewart and photographer Nick Cubbin in *The Australian Magazine*, 28–29 Apr., 2001, pp. 12–15 about persistent tensions in the Kelly country over the appropriate representation of the Kelly outbreak for tourists — the latest in a long line of such journalistic expeditions.

14 *The Weekend Australian* 19–20 May 2001, p. 5.

15 Such objects also command high prices on the collector's market. A cow horn etched with the (approximate) likenesses of the bushranger, his sister and, allegedly Constable Fitzpatrick, was sold at auction in July, 2001 for $165, 000 ($192, 225 including GST and costs), *The Age*, 19 July 2001, p. 8.

16 *The Age*, 1 Aug. 2001. Other Kelly items were also disposed of at the auction, including a transcription of the Jerilderie Letter which went to an anonymous bidder for $50 000.

17 *The Weekend Australian* 7-8 Aug. 1999.

18 ABC-TV 'Lateline', 31 Aug. 2000.

19 *Australian Financial Review Weekend* 4-5 Aug. 2001, p. 2.

20 Widely reported in the Australian media (*The West Australian*, 22 Feb., p. 41, for instance) and even in the British press (*The Daily Express*, 1 Aug. 1996, p. 14), which ever since the Kellys first broke out has followed the story with the enthusiasm of the colonialist voyeur.

21 Rose, D., *Dingo Makes Us Human: Life and Land in an Aboriginal Australian Culture*, Melbourne, 1992. I have collected similar traditions from Western Australian Aboriginal people.

22 See Seal, G., *The Outlaw Legend: A Cultural Tradition in Britain, America and Australia*, Cambridge University Press, Cambridge, 1996 and 'Deep Continuities and Discontinuities in the Outlaw Hero Traditions of Britain, America and Australia', *Lore & Language* 100, 1993.

23 Many of the works of Paterson, Lawson, their contemporaries and later emulators highlight this point, as does a good deal of our colonial folksong and ballad repertoire.

See Seal, G., *Banjo Paterson's Old Bush Songs*, Sydney, 1983; Webby, E. & Butterss, P. (eds) *The Penguin Book of Australian Ballads* and Meredith, J. & Anderson, H., *Folksongs of Australia*, Sydney, 1967 and Meredith, J., Covell, R. & Brown, P. *Folksongs of Australia Volume 2*, Kensington, 1987. See Carroll, J (ed.), *Intruders in the Bush* Melbourne, 1992 for a selection of writings that, in part, deal with these matters.

24 Seal, G., 'Jack Donohoe and the Irish Woodstove: Ambivalent Irishness in Australian Folklore', paper presented at the 13th Irish–Australian History Conference, Perth, 2000 and Seal G., 'Narrating Nation: Ned Kelly and the Ambivalence of Folk Heroism', paper presented to the 11th Congress of the International Society for Folk Narrative Research, University of Melbourne, 2001.

25 For the International Centenary of Cinema in 1995, Australia produced a series of stamps including one titled 'The Story of the Kelly Gang' as well as a prepaid post-card which featured the stamp and the original movie poster.

26 McDermott, A. (ed.), *The Jerilderie Letter by Ned Kelly*, Text Publishing, Melbourne, 2001. See also his comments in the *Eureka Street* review article, op. cit.

27 Seal, G., 'Tradition and Protest in Nineteenth Century England and Wales', *Folklore*, 100:2, 1988.

28 In April, 1994, the West Australian-based Challenge Bank began an expensive print and television advertising campaign featuring Ned Kelly making a 'withdrawal'. Although Ned's legend has only limited resonances in Western Australia, the bank's advertising agency still managed to sell this odd sales pitch.

29 Other artists have also been attracted to the Kelly legend, including Donald Friend, whose 'Hasten Edward, the Troopers are Upon Us' portrays a helmeted but other-wise palely naked Ned jumping from his bath and being handed a rifle by a fully clothed woman, was sold at auction for more than $44,000 in September, 2001. *Australian Financial Review Weekend*, 8–9 Sept. 2001, p. 37.

30 *Weekend Australian* 7–8 July 2001, p. 9.

31 Initiated by the Keating government for practical political reasons, but nevertheless taken up at the popular level, leading to the referendum on the question of a republic.

32 'Poor Ned' composed by Trevor Lucas. Contrary to my view that this song had not made an impact in oral tradition (p. 167 of the original edition), 'Poor Ned' has been recorded by numerous performers in Australia and elsewhere and is also often sung at folk music venues. Manifold's poem, which stimulated Lucas to write 'Poor Ned', was published in the poet's *The Death of Ned Kelly and Other Ballads*, London, 1941. The poem was inspired by a half-remembered fragment of lyric and melody collected by the poet, according to his notes in Manifold, J. (ed.), *The Penguin Australian Song Book*, Ringwood, 1964, p. 176.

BIBLIOGRAPHICAL NOTE

The main sources for this book are set out in the appropriate chapter notes.

Undoubtedly the best book to date on the events of 1878–80 is John McQuilton's *The Kelly Outbreak 1878–1880: The Geographical Dimension of Social Banditry* (Melbourne, 1979). Another excellent work is C. Cave (ed.), *Ned Kelly: Man and Myth* (Melbourne, 1968) which records a seminar on Ned Kelly held at Wangaratta the previous year and includes some very good papers by Ian Jones. Max Brown's *Australian Son: A Life of Ned Kelly* (Melbourne, 1948) is a fine account of the bushranger's career and J. J. Kenneally's *The Complete Inner History of the Kelly Gang and Their Pursuers* (Moe, Victoria, 1929) is an extremely partisan but fascinating glimpse into the heart of the Kelly country through a man who knew many of the surviving participants of the outbreak. Clive Turnbull's *Kellyana* (Melbourne, 1943) is also well worth a look for the many works on Kelly and his legend up to the 1940s.

The most extensive, single mass of primary information about the Kellys, their friends, the police and aspects of the outbreak is the *Police Commission: Minutes of Evidence Taken Before the Royal Commission on the Police Force of Victoria, 1881*, conveniently available in a Pioneer Facsimile Edition (Adelaide, 1968). The Kelly Papers in the Public Records Office of Victoria are the most important collection of relevant documents. Significant slices of the Victorian Crown

Lands Commission can be found in J. M. Powell (ed.), *Yeoman and Bureaucrats: The Victorian Crown Lands Commission, 1878–1879* (London, 1973).

Readers interested in oral traditions associated with the Kellys are referred to the John Meredith Tape Collection in the National Library, Canberra, a portion of which has been published by J. Meredith and H. Anderson as *Folksongs of Australia* (Melbourne, 1967), and to Warren Fahey's Australian Folklore Unit tapes, also housed in the National Library. A selection of material from this collection is available commercially on LP disc *Bush Traditions* (Larrikin Records, LRF 007, Sydney, 1976). Max Brown's book also contains some interesting material of this kind as does the work of folklore collector Ron Edwards, whose published material is most accessible in *The Big Book of Australian Folk Song* (Sydney, 1976).

The initial impetus for historians to study banditry seriously came with publication of Eric Hobsbawm's *Primitive Rebels* (Manchester, 1959) which included a chapter on what he termed 'Social Bandits'. This was followed by a book titled *Social Bandits* (London, 1969), since reprinted as *Bandits*.

In fact, anthropologists and folklorists had been studying banditry in various forms for many years and Hobsbawm's main contribution was to offer a synthesis of the observed data within a cross-cultural conceptual framework. Invaluable though this has been for study of an area neglected by historians, it has become quite obvious that Hobsbawm's criteria for social bandits do not apply very well in the context of literate pre-industrial and post-industrial societies like Australia and the United States. This is not really surprising considering that Hobsbawm's exemplary data were drawn largely from peasant cultures. It seems to me that the concept of the highwayman tradition briefly outlined in this book is a more useful perspective on the Anglo-Saxon experience of banditry and has the additional advantage of relating various kinds of traditional expressive material to specific occurrences and motivations of agrarian protest.

It should also be mentioned that Hobsbawm's theories have not found favour with all anthropologists. Anton Blok's 'The Peasant and the Brigand: Social Banditry Reconsidered' *(Comparative Studies in Society and History*, vol. 14, no. 4, 1972), for example, takes issue with

Hobsbawm on the topic of Sicilian banditry and is ably parried by Hobsbawm in 'Social Banditry: Reply' (*Comparative Studies in Society and History*, vol. 14, no. 4, 1972). Blok's full-length study, *The Mafia of a Sicilian Village* (Oxford, 1974) is also relevant here, as is Gavin Maxwell's book on the life of Salvatore Guiliano, the Sicilian outlaw, titled *God Protect Me From My Friends* (London, 1956). Guiliano's story has some very interesting similarities to Ned Kelly's saga.

Australian bushranging has had no shortage of chroniclers, beginning with James Bonwick's *The Bushrangers: Illustrating the Early Days of Van Diemen's Land* (Melbourne, 1856) and including Charles White, George Boxall, and even Jack Bradshaw, the self-proclaimed 'Last of the Bushrangers'. Charles White's *History of Australian Bushranging*, published in a variety of forms since 1893, has become, despite its chronological and other inaccuracies, the only approximation to a standard work.

In the past, academic historians tended to treat bushranging with disinterest or disdain, concentrating on separating the 'facts' from the fiction or folklore. An exception was Russel Ward whose *The Australian Legend* (London, 1958) included a serious discussion of bushranging and Australian folklore in general. Unfortunately, Ward's book has been seen as the last word on the subject rather than the excellent pioneering work it actually is.

With the publication of the results of the Wangaratta Seminar as *Ned Kelly: Man or Myth*, and some recent extensions of the ideas presented in that book by McQuilton, and D. Morrissey's 'Ned Kelly's Sympathisers' (*Historical Studies,* vol. 18, Oct. 1978) there is a growing awareness that the fiction or folklore may be just as significant as the facts, perhaps even more so. It has certainly been established that bushranging is an important indicator of agrarian tensions and, for that reason alone, deserves close attention, preferably from an interdisciplinary point of view.

The following is a selection of relevant works that have appeared since the original edition of this book was published:

Balcarek, D., *Ellen Kelly*, Glenrowan, 1984.
Bedford, J., *Sister Kate*, Ringwood, 1982.

Carey, P., *True History of the Kelly Gang*, Brisbane, 2000.

Drewe, R., *Our Sunshine*, Ringwood, 1992.

Dunstan, K., *Saint Ned: The Story of the Near-Sanctification of an Australian Outlaw*, Sydney, 1980.

Jones, I., *Ned Kelly: A Short Life* , Port Melbourne, 1995.

Jones, I., *The Friendship that Destroyed Ned Kelly: Joe Byrne and Aaron Sherritt*, Port Melbourne, 1992.

McDermott, A. (ed.), *The Jerilderie Letter by Ned Kelly*, Melbourne, 2001.

Meredith, J., Covell, R. & Brown, P. (eds.), *Folksongs of Australia Volume 2*, Sydney, 1987.

Molony, J., *I Am Ned Kelly*, Ringwood, 1981.

Phillips, J., *The Trial of Ned Kelly*, Sydney, 1987.

Powell, G., *Ned Kelly Country*, Robert Brown & Associates, 1997.

Reece, R. (ed.), *Exiles from Erin: Convict Lives in Ireland and Australia*, Basingstoke, 1991.

Rose, D., *Dingo Makes Us Human: Life and Land in an Aboriginal Australian Culture*, Melbourne, 1992.

Seal, G., 'Deep Continuities and Discontinuities in the Outlaw Hero Traditions of Britain, America and Australia', *Lore & Language* 100, 1993.

Seal, G., *The Outlaw Legend: A Cultural Tradition in Britain, America and Australia*, Cambridge University Press, Cambridge, 1996.

Webby, E. & Butterss, P. (eds.) *The Penguin Book of Australian Ballads*, rev. edn. Ringwood, 1993.

INDEX